CRAFT it now

75+ Simple Handmade Projects

Edited by Shannon E. Miller

KP CRAFT
CINCINNATI, OHIO

Contents

There you are, enjoying a normal Saturday afternoon at home, when it hits you—the sudden, inexplicable urge to MAKE something.

Sound familiar? It sure does to me. For as long as I can remember, this creative impulse has been a driving force behind my weekend plans, free evenings and even lunch breaks. And while more time-consuming projects are always in the works, sometimes I just need a simple how-to to take the edge off of this crazy itch to craft. At times like these, I head straight to my craft library: a set of shelves where I store a variety of thick, multi-craft compilation books, both vintage and new.

Much like a favorite cookbook that is referred to time and again for fresh meal ideas as well as old favorites, these craft books are like old friends that always know what to serve when I'm in need of an inspirational jolt. They're on standby for when I am feeling a little

Introduction

adventurous for a bite-size taste of something I've never tried before, without making me feel like I'm in over my head; and they always deliver when I want to go back to basics with a genre I've already mastered.

Whether you have a similar craft book collection, or are seeking the perfect way to start one, this book is a must-have addition. Bursting with dozens of handpicked, easy-to-follow tutorials for simple projects with contemporary style, it is bound to be your new go-to resource for gifts, accessories and home décor projects that span sewing and embroidery, to paper and yarn crafts, jewelry, felt and even a bit of upcycling.

Feeling bold? Don't hold yourself back by the constraints of the suggested supply lists or instructional steps; let them be merely a starting point for your project ideas. The sky is the limit! Make each item your own by switching up the colors, putting a different spin on a simple technique or mixing it up by combining elements from different projects into one. (I like to call this "Frankencrafting"—sometimes a little scary, but often, surprisingly successful!)

So go ahead, clear your afternoon—let's get crafty!

The Projects

Heirloom Tomato Pincushion
by Angela Davis

Inspired by the piles of heirloom tomatoes found at farmers' markets, this pincushion also reminds me of the tomato pincushions in the sewing baskets of my mother and grandmother.

MATERIALS

One 7" (17.8cm) square of wool felt in red, yellow, light green, beige or any other color you prefer for the body of your tomato

One 4" (10.2cm) square of wool felt in medium to dark green for the stem and top

A few yards of strong carpet or button thread

¾ oz. (21.3g) wool roving or polyester fiberfill (wool roving is recommended since the lanolin in the wool will keep your pins rust free and sharp)

Craft glue

1 Using the appropriate templates and felt, cut out the tomato body, stem and top. With sharp scissors, make a scant ½" (1.3cm) snip right in the middle of your tomato top.

2 Using strong carpet thread or button thread, thread a needle, knot one end and make running stitches around the perimeter of the tomato circle, about ⅛" (3mm) from the edge. The longer your stitches, the more asymmetrical your tomato will be. Pull the thread to create a ball-like shape. Do not tie off yet.

3 Stuff the tomato, packing it in firmly.

4 Tack the tomato closed with a few stitches. The edges will not come all the way together, but this will be covered by the top. Knot a few times, but do cut the thread.

5 Fold the stem piece in half to make a loop. Tack the bottom edges together and to the top of the tomato. Knot the thread and tie off, snipping the excess thread.

6 Place the top onto the tomato, pulling the stem loop through the small cut in the top. Glue the points of the top to the tomato. Let the very tips curl up a bit for a more authentic look. Let the glue dry, then stick in some pins.

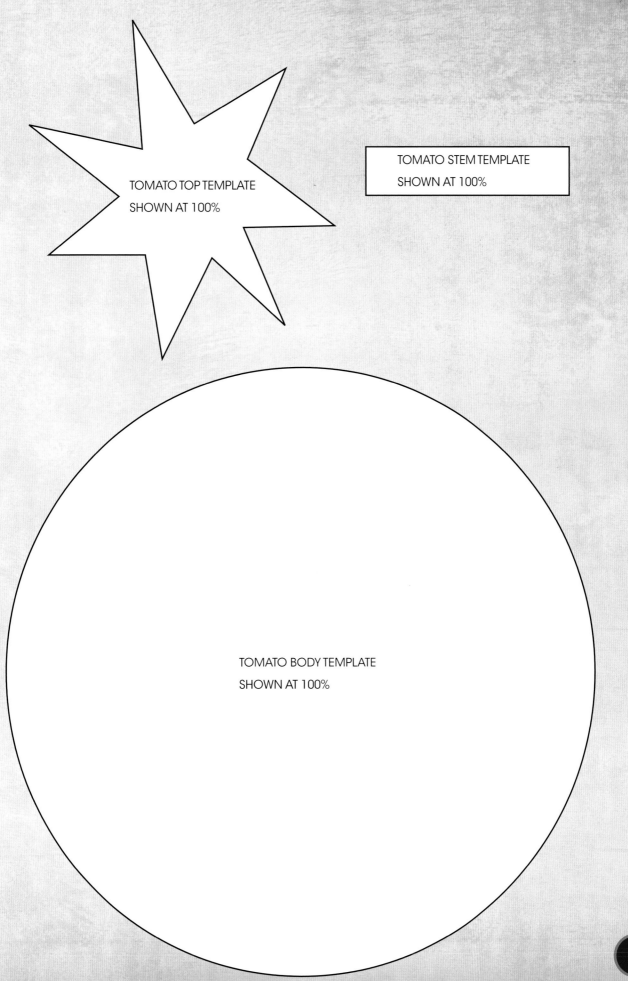

TOMATO TOP TEMPLATE

SHOWN AT 100%

TOMATO STEM TEMPLATE

SHOWN AT 100%

TOMATO BODY TEMPLATE

SHOWN AT 100%

Polymer Clay Buttons
by Anne Glynis Davies

This is a great project to get familiar with polymer clay. Use your finished buttons to decorate a greeting card or a scrapbook page—even sew them onto a bag or scarf. Have fun!

MATERIALS

Variety of 2 oz. (56g) polymer clay blocks

Clay blade or sharp knife

Acrylic rod or brayer; a wine bottle or glass tumbler are suitable alternatives

Mini cookie cutters in a variety of shapes (square, circle, triangle, heart, leaf, etc.)

Cocktail sticks or a knitting needle (for making holes)

Optional: water-based gloss varnish; cardstock, needle and thread

1 Preheat oven according to the polymer clay manufacturer's instructions.Cut a piece of clay in a chosen color. Soften the clay by working it in your hands: push on it, pull it, roll it into a ball and flatten it out again until the clay becomes pliable. If there are air pockets in the clay (visible bumps on the surface), pierce them, and press the clay with your fingers to get the air out.

2 Blend the clay with smaller amounts of other colors to create a marbled effect. Experiment to get a pleasing pattern—this is all part of the fun.

3 Flatten the softened clay out on your work surface with a roller until it is at least ⅜" (1cm) thick. Cut out the button with a mini cookie cutter and peel away the excess clay. Poke 2 or 4 holes into your button with a cocktail stick, moving it in tiny circles to slightly widen the hole.

4 If your work surface is a ceramic tile, place it straight in an electric oven. Otherwise, transfer the button to a baking sheet by sliding a knife gently underneath it and placing the button on the baking sheet. Never put polymer clay in a gas oven or a microwave. Bake for about 30 minutes, or as instructed. Baking times may vary between brands of polymer clay.

5 Allow the button to cool. Optional: Apply a coat of water-based gloss varnish to make your button extra resistant to wear and laundering. The varnish is completely dry after 24 hours.

6 Optional: Make a presentation card for your button. Cut a piece of cardstock into a 2¾" × 3½" (7cm × 8.9cm) rectangle. Decorate your presentation card with distress inks, spray paints or marker pens; add a border effect using raffia or yarns, as desired. Write a message on the back of your card to say that the button is handmade and suggest how it can be used. Stitch the button to the card with the decorated side facing you.

Note
Store any unused clay in baking parchment or polyethylene bags away from sunlight. Clean your tools with baby wipes.

Button Handmade by:
...... Anne ......
Use me to decorate a greetings card, a scrapbook page, a journal or a photo album.
Why not sew me onto a bag, scarf or even a pair of slippers?
Have fun!

Beaded Pin

by Barbara Swanson

This retro inspired pin is the perfect accent for any outfit. Memory Thread helps shape this circular design, but also works well with other shapes.

MATERIALS

Two 2" (5.1cm) squares of light blue Ultrasuede

DMC Color Infusions Memory Thread*

75 to 100 crystal seed beads

Nylon thread

Embroidery floss*

1" (2.5cm) circle of buckram

Craft glue

¾" (1.9cm) pin back

*Note
For this project, I used Memory Thread color no. 6360 and DMC Embroidery Floss no. 800.

1 Draw a 1⅛" (2.9cm) circle on the center of one of the Ultrasuede squares.

2 Shape the Memory Thread in a tight circular/spiral shape, crimping ¼" (6mm) of the end under at the center so it won't show.

3 String 10 to 15 beads on the nylon thread. Starting at the center of the circle, couch the Memory Thread and the beads (threaded on the nylon thread) in place using one strand of the floss. Sew 1 or 2 beads in place along with the Memory Thread for each couched section. Thread more beads as needed. Work toward the outer edge of the circle, crimping the end of the Memory Thread under ¼" (6mm) to create a smooth edge.

4 Carefully trim the stitched piece and center and adhere the buckram to the wrong side.

5 Cut a circle the same size as the stitched piece from the remaining square of Ultrasuede. Center and adhere with craft glue to cover the buckram.

6 Adhere the pin back in place at the back.

Patchwork Garden Party Invitation
by Benetta Strydom

This invitation is perfect for any tea party occasion, from a kitchen tea for a bride-to-be to a birthday party for a mother or grandmother.

MATERIALS

6⅔" × 9⅔" (16.9cm × 24.5cm) piece of light blue marbled cardstock

Fine paintbrush

Gray, white and light pink acrylic paint

Teacup stamp*

Two 2" (5.1cm) squares of dark blue sugar paper

2" (5.1cm) square of white sugar paper

Three 2" (5.1cm) squares of pink sugar paper

Fine felt-tip pen

6 small flat-sided rhinestone beads

Quick-drying glue

Note
I used Jablos teacup stamp G035.

1 Score the marbled cardstock in half to create a card.

2 Use the paintbrush to apply an even layer of the white paint on the stamp. Stamp the image onto the blue sugar paper square, and then carefully lift the stamp. Repeat with the remaining paper squares, stamping white paint on blue squares, pink paint on the white square and gray paint on pink squares. Clean the stamp before starting the next color by repeatedly dabbing it onto a scrap piece of paper until it is clean.

3 With the fold at the left, center and then glue the 6 sugar paper squares onto the front of the card.

4 Use the pen to draw stitches onto the patchwork design.

5 Glue a rhinestone bead to the center of each teacup's flower.

Hazy Mazy Runner
by Barbara Gaddy

Perfect for tabletops, this *Hazy Mazy Runner* makes use of fat quarters, allowing you to experiment with fabric and color.

MATERIALS

4 coordinating fat quarters*

26" (66cm) square of batting

1 yd (2.9m) of fabric (for backing and binding)

CUTTING INSTRUCTIONS

From each fat quarter (A, B, C and D), cut the following:

Two 6½" × 2½" (16.5cm × 6.4cm) (8 total)

Three 2½" (6.4cm) squares (12 total)

Eight 1½" (3.8cm) (32 total)

From the 8 strips cut:

> Thirteen: 6½" × 1½" (16.5cm × 3.8cm)
>
> Two 1½" (3.8cm) squares
>
> Two 2½" × 1½" (6.4cm × 3.8cm)
>
> Two 3½" × 1½" (8.9cm × 3.8cm)
>
> Two 4½" × 1½" (11.4cm × 3.8cm)
>
> Two 5½" × 1½" (14cm × 3.8cm)

*Notes

A fat quarter is a piece of fabric usually measuring 18" × 22" (45.7cm × 55.9cm). Fat quarters are sold precut in most fabric stores.

Use ¼" (6mm) seams.

Center Blocks

1 Make the center blocks: Sew three 2½" (6.4cm) squares together, in A B A pattern (Figure A).

2 Sew two 6½" × 2½" (16.5cm × 6.4cm) strips to the top and bottom of the A B A block, using the same fabric A for the side strips (Figure B). Repeat steps 1 and 2 until you have 4 blocks, making each block a different fabric combination.

3 Sew the 4 center blocks together to create the Center Four-Patch unit (Figure C).

Log Cabin Blocks

1 Make the Log Cabin blocks: Sew two 1½" (3.8cm) squares together from fabric A and B. Then sew the 2½" × 1½" (6.4cm × 3.8cm) strip from fabric B to the side. Next, sew a 2½" × 1½" (6.4cm × 3.8cm) strip from fabric C to the bottom, followed by a 3½" × 1½" (8.9cm × 3.8cm) strip to the side from fabric C. Next, sew the 3½" × 1½" (8.9cm × 3.8cm) piece from fabric D to the bottom, then a 4½" × 1½" (11.4cm × 3.8cm) strip from fabric D to the side. Sew a 4½" × 1½" (11.4cm × 3.8cm) strip from fabric A to the bottom, followed by a 5½" × 1½" (14cm × 3.8cm) strip from fabric A to the side. Sew a 5½" × 1½" (14cm × 3.8cm) strip from fabric B to the bottom, followed by a 6½" × 1½" (16.5cm × 3.8cm) strip from fabric B to the side (Figure D). Repeat—alternating the color scheme—until you have 4 blocks.

Strip Rows

1 Sew twelve 6½" × 1½" (16.5cm × 3.8cm) strips together lengthwise, in any order. Repeat until you have four 12-Strip Rows.

2 Sew one 12-Strip Row to the top of the Center Four Patch unit, and one 12-Strip Row to the bottom.

3 To create the side rows, sew the two Log Cabin blocks to each end of the remaining 12-Strip Rows.

4 Sew the side rows to the sides of the Center Four Patch section (Figure E).

5 Add the batting and backing. Quilt as desired, then bind.

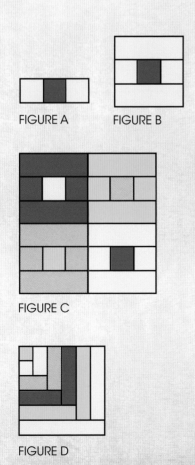

FIGURE A   FIGURE B

FIGURE C

FIGURE D

FIGURE E

Felt Flower Wreath
by Andretta Ross

This wreath can be made in colors to suit any decor, season, or holiday. For use outdoors, use eco-friendly felt. Made from 100 percent recycled bottles and plastics, the felt is practically fade proof.

MATERIALS

2 yds (1.8m) felt

12" (30.5cm) straw wreath form

Hot glue gun and hot glue sticks

1 Cut a strip from the felt about 3" (7.6cm) wide. Wrap the felt strip around the wreath and glue the ends down. If your strip isn't long enough to cover the wreath from, cut another stip and wrap until the form is covered. This creates a nice, secure base for the flowers and also makes the back of the wreath attractive. Set the wreath aside.

2 Use the template to cut out 70 to 80 felt circles.

3 Make the circle into a flower: Start with your scissors at the bottom of the circle and cut in a counterclockwise spiral until there is a small circle left in the middle (the dotted line on the template shows where to cut).

4 Make the spiral into a flower: Roll the spiral in on itself, starting from the outside point of the circle where you first started cutting. Roll until you reach the small circle at the end. Glue the small circle onto the bottom of the rolled flower to secure it. Repeat with the remaing felt circles.

5 Lay the wrapped wreath form on a flat surface and glue the felt flowers to the surface, leaving the back uncovered so that the wreath will hang flat. Continue gluing flowers onto the wreath until the front and sides are completely covered.

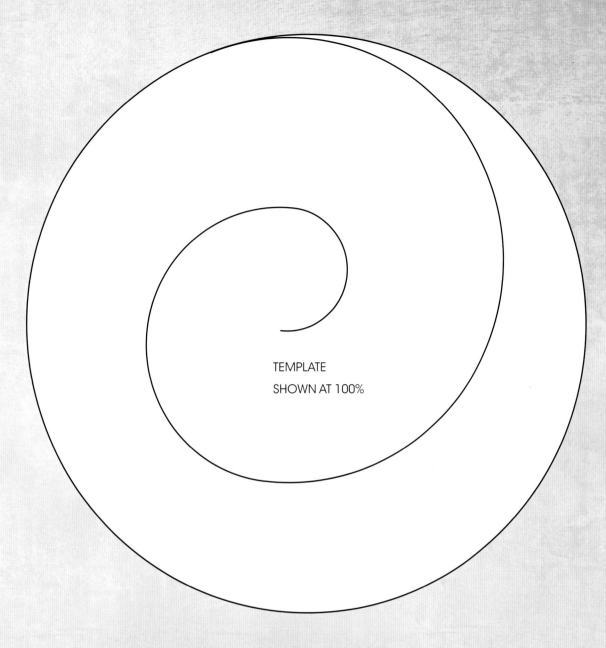

TEMPLATE

SHOWN AT 100%

Easy Fringed Scarf
by Beth Major

This easy-to-make, easy-to-wear scarf is a great last-minute gift, and is the perfect winter accessory.

MATERIALS

2 balls Loops & Threads Charisma (109 yds/100m) or any similar bulky weight yarn; shown in color Forest

Size US L (8mm) crochet hook

GAUGE

9 hdc and 7 rows = 4" (10cm)

1 Cut 36 strands of yarn 12" (30.5cm) long for the fringe and set aside.

2 Crochet the scarf using the pattern below.

Row 1: Create a slipknot leaving approximately a 6" (15.2cm) tail then ch 13, turn, hdc in third ch from hook and in each ch across.
Row 2: Ch 2, turn, hdc in first hdc and in each hdc across, hdc into next ch (12 hdc).
Row 3: Ch 2, turn, hdc in first hdc and in each hdc across (12 hdc).

Repeat row 3 until the scarf measures about 70" (1.8m). Ch 1, cut the yarn, and pull through the last ch stitch. Weave in the ends.

3 Add the fringe: Take 3 strands of yarn at a time (from the strands set aside) and carefully fold the strands in half. Insert the fold through a stitch at the end of the scarf, bring the ends through the fold and snug down firmly. Do this approximately every second stitch. Repeat for other end of scarf. Trim the ends of the fringe to approximately 5" (12.7cm) or so it looks even.

Personal Message Flower Pot
by Dalia Torres

Turn old clay pots into beautiful message flower pots to inspire all who view them. The chalkboard paint allows you to change the message whenever you want. These pots make great gifts.

MATERIALS

Clay pot

Old newspaper or other paper sheets (to protect area from paint)

Spray paint

Chalkboard paint or chalkboard vinyl label

Chalk or liquid chalk marker

1 Make sure that your clay pot is clean and dry. Cover your work area with newspaper.

2 Place the pot upside down with the open rim on the bottom. Spray the pot evenly, being careful not to oversaturate the pot. You may have to give it 2 coats, depending on your pot. Let the pot dry for about an hour.

3 Once the pot is dry, add a chalkboard vinyl label or chalkboard paint to your pot. Make sure the label is the correct size for your pot. If using chalkboard paint, let the paint dry 48 to 72 hours before writing on it.

4 Now your pot is ready for your gardening messages. Write your message with chalk or a liquid chalk marker.

Plush Chocolate Bunny
by Cheryl Bush

Make a *Plush Chocolate Bunny* to fill an Easter basket or decorate the house for spring. This sweet little guy is cute, cuddly and best of all, sugar free!

MATERIALS

⅜ yd (34.3cm) brown velour knit fabric

6" × 12" (15.2cm × 30.5cm) piece of tear-away stabilizer (type used for embroidery)

Brown thread

Polyester fiberfill

Hand sewing needle

Small scrap of yellow felt

Blue button

14" (35.6cm) piece of ribbon

Note
Use a ½" (1.3cm) allowance. A ball point sewing machine needle works best for this project.

1 Transfer the template onto paper and cut out. Fold the velour fabric in half, with the selvages together. Pin the pattern piece to the fabric, parallel to the selvage and cut out. Transfer the pattern markings for the ears, legs and eye to the right side of the fabric.

2 Cut the tear-away stabilizer into three 2" × 6" (5.1cm × 15.2cm) strips. Pin the stabilizer strips to the back of the fabric behind the markings for the topstitching. Satin stitch (a wide, close together machine zigzag) over the marking lines with the brown thread, stitching slowly so the fabric does not stretch and the stitching looks nice and smooth.

3 With the right sides of the velour fabric facing, pin the bunny halves together all the way around. Stitch together around the edge with a straight stitch, leaving a 1"–2" (2.5cm–5.1cm) gap at the bottom for turning. Trim down the seam allowance, clipping around curves, being careful not to clip through the stitching.

4 Turn the bunny right side out and use a pencil or a knitting needle to gently poke out the corners and curves. Stuff with the fiberfill, using the pencil or needle to stuff into all edges until plumply filled. Pin the raw edges of the opening inward.

5 Hand-stitch the opening closed with a slip stitch. Cut a circle from the yellow felt that is just slightly bigger than the blue button. Layer the button over the felt circle and place on the eye marking on the bunny. Hand-stitch the button and felt circle onto the bunny to create the eye. Tie the ribbon around the bunny's neck and make a bow.

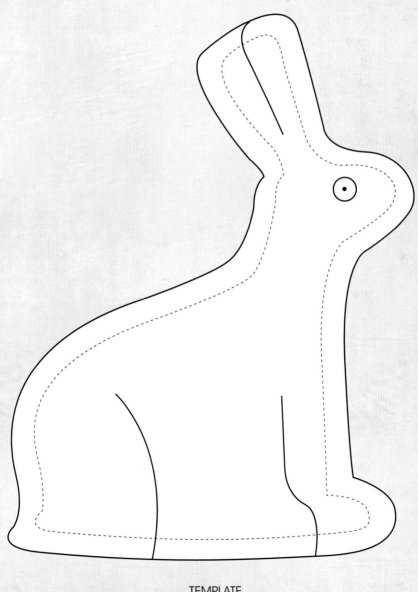

TEMPLATE

SHOWN AT 50%

Camping Embroidery Trio
by Courtney Kyle

These three miniature embroideries feature camping motifs, perfect for the outdoor enthusiast.

MATERIALS

Optional: water-based wood stain

Three 3" (7.6cm) wooden embroidery hoops

White linen

Embroidery floss in black, red, burnt orange and teal (or as preferred)

Craft glue

1 Optional: To add some rustic color to your embroidery hoops, stain them using a water-based stain. Let dry for at least 1 hour before hooping fabric.

2 With fabric secured in embroidery hoops, center and trace the embroidery designs.

3 Backstitch the embroidery designs and trim the excess fabric off the back of each hoop.

4 Unhoop the embroideries, iron them and apply a bead of glue to the hoops before rehooping.

TENT TEMPLATE
SHOWN AT 100%

FIRE TEMPLATE
SHOWN AT 100%

BIKE TEMPLATE
SHOWN AT 100%

Fabric Flower Corsage
by Christen Barber

This fabric flower corsage adds a pop of color to a bag, headband or dress—the uses are endless!

MATERIALS

2" (5.1cm) x width of fabric (approximately 40" [101.6cm]) strip of fabric

Needle and thread

Jeweled button

Craft glue

Glue-on clasp back pin

1 Fold one of the short ends of your fabric strip wrong sides together about a ½" (1.3cm). Place 2 stitches to hold in place about ¼" (6mm) from the bottom edge.

2 Use a long running straight stitch ¼" (6mm) from the bottom along the entire length of the fabric strip (40" [101.6cm] long side), gathering the fabric as you go. When you reach the end, be sure to pull the gathered fabric tight and keep the needle and thread in place.

3 Using the folded end of the fabric strip as the center of your flower, wrap the rest of the gathered strip around it to create the flower. Stitch all layers together with a needle and thread to hold the flower shape in place. Once sturdy and complete, knot the thread and cut.

4 Glue the jeweled button in the center of the flower. Once the glue is dry, glue the pin clasp onto the back of the flower. Let dry completely before wearing.

Fall Foliage Coaster
by Dian K. Wardhani

This simple coaster is perfect for a fall-time tabletop. Make a full set of coasters, or string them together for a festive garland.

MATERIALS

3 shades of green felt

Thin foam (for batting)

Embroidery thread

Cotton ribbon

Button

1 Cut out the leaf pieces and batting using the templates.

2 Pin the 3 top leaf pieces onto the batting, and, using a running stitch, sew the pieces to the batting along the interior edges.

3 Fold the ribbon in half, and place the ends behind the top piece. Place the button on the right side of the top piece, over the ribbon, and sew on, sewing through the ribbon.

4 Lay the front piece on top of the back piece, right side up. Blanket-stitch all the way around the edge. Fasten thread.

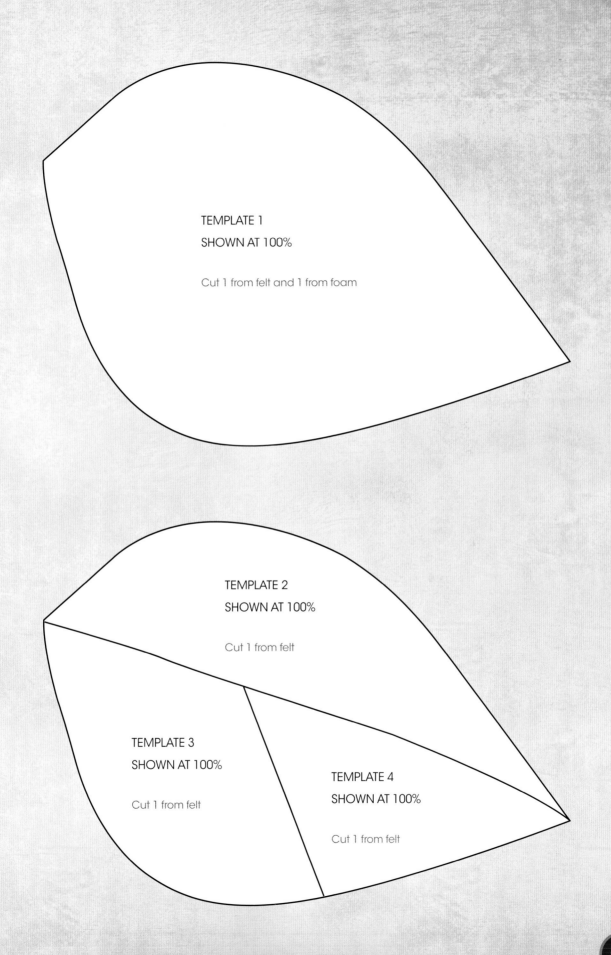

TEMPLATE 1
SHOWN AT 100%

Cut 1 from felt and 1 from foam

TEMPLATE 2
SHOWN AT 100%

Cut 1 from felt

TEMPLATE 3
SHOWN AT 100%

Cut 1 from felt

TEMPLATE 4
SHOWN AT 100%

Cut 1 from felt

Snapshots of Nature Mini Album
by Katie Smith

Fill this album with photos from a recent trip, or use it as a place to store pictures that inspire you.

MATERIALS

5 sheets double-sided paper in different patterns

Hole punch

3 rolls of washi tape

4 pieces of ribbon

Assorted stickers

Assorted nature photos (your own or cut from magazines)

Brush pen

Adhesive tape

1 Use the template to cut sheets of double-sided patterned paper into tags.

2 Punch a hole into the top of each patterned paper tag. Line the edges of each tag with washi tape.

3 Bind the tags together by threading ribbons through the holes of all 9 tags and tie them closed leaving about 1½" (3.8cm) of slack.

4 Add photos and embellish with patterned papers, washi tape, stickers and doodles. Label your photos.

Punch hole here

TEMPLATE

SHOWN AT 100%

Beginner's Belt

by Danielle Branch

The design for this belt is simple and familiar; however, both the belt and the D-rings are crocheted. Use acrylic or cotton yarn for the best results.

MATERIALS

White cotton or white acrylic yarn (for belt)

Black yarn or other contrasting color (for D-rings)

Size US J (6mm) crochet hook

Size US G (4.25mm) crochet hook

GAUGE

Gauge is not critical to this project. Chain the number of stitches necessary to fit around your waist plus a little extra for the looping through the D-rings.

1 Crochet the belt using the pattern below.

Belt

With hook J and white yarn, ch 100 sts, or enough to wrap around your waist with a little extra. Turn.

Rnd 1: Skip the first 2 ch sts, and sc in each of the next 98 ch sts (or number needed for your size). Continue working along the opposite side of ch, sc in each ch. Sl st to join.

Work 2 more rounds in BLO. Finish off.

D-rings

Wrap the black yarn around 2 fingers held together 7 times (you will create a circle of yarn).

Sc around the wrapped yarn, about 14 stitches (enough to cover the ring). Sl st to join.

Make 2.

2 Assemble the belt as follows. Hold the 2 D-rings together, and with hook G and contrast color, sc 6 times through both rings until the rings are joined.

Fold 1 end of the belt over the D-rings, covering the 6 sc where the rings are joined. Sew the end of the belt down to secure.

Linen Appliqué Ornament
by Joy Niehaus

Be sure to pick a fabric with a somewhat large motif that you can easily fussy cut for the appliqué.

MATERIALS

Iron-on adhesive (such as Wonder Under, or Steam-a-Seam)

Scrap of fabric with an interesting design to fussy cut (for appliqué)

5" (12.7cm) square of linen fabric

5" (12.7cm) square of coordinating fabric (for backing)

5" (12.7cm) square of medium weight, sew-in interfacing

6" (15.2cm) ribbon

1 Cut the iron-on adhesive into 3 squares: 1 to fit the size of your appliqué fabric and two 5" (12.7cm) squares. Iron-on adhesive has a paper side and an exposed side. One at a time, place the exposed side of the adhesive to the wrong side of your fabric pieces and iron for 3 to 5 seconds. Let fabric cool. Draw a 3½" (8.9cm) circle onto the right side of the linen fabric.

2 Cut out the desired appliqué design. This is a great way to use scrap fabric and fabrics with small details. Remove the paper backing from fabric appliqué and place it in the center of the circle you drew on the linen. Iron over appliqué for 3 to 5 seconds using constant pressure. Turn the linen over and iron the back side for a 3 to 5 seconds.

3 Remove the paper from the backing fabric and place it right side up on the interfacing. Iron fabric for 3 to 5 seconds then turn it over and iron the backing for 3 to 5 seconds. Remove the paper

backing from the linen square and place it right side up on the interfacing. Iron for 3 to 5 seconds. You should now have a sandwich with the backing fabric, interfacing and linen fabric. The right sides of the fabrics should be facing outward. Cut out the circle staying just inside the line you drew on the linen fabric.

4 Pull back the linen fabric at the top of your ornament. Fold the ribbon in half and slip the ends inside. Fold the linen back into place. Using your sewing machine, stitch around the edge of your circle staying as close to the edge as possible and being sure to sew through all layers, including the ribbon. Stitch around the inside of the appliqué staying as close to the edge as possible. (Use copordinating threads for a more subtle look and contrasting thread for a bolder look.)

Hang on your Christmas tree, attach to a gift, or add to hooks for a personal, festive touch.

Decorative Sewing Pins
by Ellyn Zinsmeister

Making your own pretty sewing pins is easy and fun. These are decorative pins to spice up your pincushion, not intended for actual use in sewing. Include them with a handmade pincushion for an extra-special gift.

MATERIALS

Shrink plastic

Permanent markers in a variety of colors

Paper punches in fun shapes

Steel sewing pins (without plastic heads)

A potato (for baking pins)

1 Preheat the oven to 350 degrees. Color sections of the shrink plastic with permanent markers and let dry completely.

2 Punch shapes out of the colored shrink plastic with the paper punches. Flowers, butterflies, leaves, hearts and stars work well.

3 Poke a straight pin through the center of the plastic shape. Push the plastic shape up so it is flush with the head of the pin. Repeat with the remaining pins.

4 Cut a potato in half. Put the potato cut side down on a flat cookie sheet and stick the pins into the potato. You can make several pins at once.

5 Bake the pins for 1–3 minutes, until the shapes shrink up and lay flat on the pin head (watch closely!).

6 Let the pins cool and share with friends.

The Weekend Scarf
by Denise Lavoie

While it takes only a weekend to complete, you'll want to wear this lace scarf all the time! A simple two-row pattern forms the crochet lace, subtle sequins add casual glamour, and fringe completes the sophisticated look.

MATERIALS

3 skeins Rowan Kidsilk Haze Glamour (177 yds/162m) or similar fingering weight yarn; shown in color Trance 284

Size US 7 (4.5mm) crochet hook

GAUGE

Working in Lace Stitch, 2½ pattern repeats over 9 rows = 4" (10.2cm)

1 Crochet the scarf using the pattern below.

Scarf

Ch 36, *[(2dc, ch 1, 2dc) in 4th ch from hook, sk 2 ch, (sc, ch 5, sc) in next ch, sk 2 ch]. Repeat from * across, ending with dc in final ch. Turn.

Work 2-row lace stitch pattern until scarf measures 64" (1.6m).

Lace Stitch Pattern:

Row 1: Ch 3, *(sc, ch 5, sc) in next ch-1 sp, (2 dc, ch 1, 2 dc) in next ch-5 sp. Repeat from * across row. Turn.

Row 2: Ch 3, *(2 dc, ch 1, 2 dc) in next ch-5 sp, (sc, ch 5, sc) in next ch-1 sp. Repeat from * across row. Turn.

Final row: Ch 5, sl st in next ch-1 sp, *ch 2, sl st in next ch-5 sp, ch 2, sl st in next ch-1 sp. Repeat from * across row, ending with ch 2, sl st in top of turning ch 3. Fasten off.

Weave in any ends and wet-block to the given dimensions.

2 Make the fringe: Cut seventy-eight 12" (30.5cm) pieces of yarn. Divide the yarn into 26 bundles of 3, folding in half so that each bundle is 6" (15.2cm) long.

Using the crochet hook, attach 13 yarn bundles evenly spaced across each short end of scarf as follows: work hook from WS to RS of scarf at spot of fringe placement, pull fringe bundle with hook at fold from RS to WS, pull fringe ends through bundle fold until taught. Once all fringe bundles are attached, fold scarf in half widthwise and trim fringe even.

Tomato Hand Needle Cushion
by Paula Ginder

An adapation of the traditional pincushion, this cushion is perfect for keeping your hand needles organized and sharp.

MATERIALS

Inkjet fabric sheet

Two 2¼" × 10" (5.7cm × 25.4cm) pieces of red wool felt

Two 10" (25.4cm) pieces of baby rickrack

Fabric glue

Heavy thread

Cotton batting

Crushed walnut shells

White DMC Pearl Cotton floss size 5

Two 3½" (8.9cm) squares of green wool felt

Small button

Leaf ribbon

Paper flower

Note
Use a ¼" (6mm) seam allowance.

1 Using your computer, create a hand needle description to go around the cushion (see Figure 1). The band should measure 1" × 10" (2.5cm × 25.4cm). Print the band onto the inkjet fabric sheet. Cut out the band.

2 Machine sew lengthwise a piece of red wool felt to the bottom of the needle band and the other piece of red wool felt to the top. Press seams open. Flip over to the right side, and using fabric glue, apply the baby rickrack on the stitch lines. Let dry.

3 Fold the piece in half with right sides together and match up the short ends. Stitch the ends together.

4 With heavy thread, hand sew a running stitch along the bottom and pull the thread to cinch together. Tack together with a couple of stitches and knot.

5 Turn the tomato right-side out. Place a piece of cotton batting on the bottom and around the sides before filling. Fill with crushed walnut shells and add another piece of cotton batting at the top. Sew a running stitch along the top, cinch and tack together just as you did for the bottom.

6 Thread the cotton floss onto a large needle. Start at the bottom center and come up through the top center, wrapping the floss around to the bottom center of the pincushion and separating the needle description. Continue until you have divided the 6 sections. You will end with your thread coming out at the top. Leave the needle threaded, it will be used to attach the tomato cap.

7 Cut out 2 tomato caps from the green wool felt. Optional: You can blanket-stitch around the caps with matching embroidery floss. Take the threaded needle with the floss and go through the center of each tomato cap. Add a button to your thread and go back down through the other hole on the button, through the tomato caps ending up at the bottom of your pincushion. Pull tight and secure the thread.

8 Glue your leaf ribbon and paper flower on top of the button. You are now ready to keep your hand needles organized!

APPLIQUÉ	BEADING	BETWEENS	CHENILLE	EMBROIDERY	SHARPS

Sample needle band

FIGURE 1

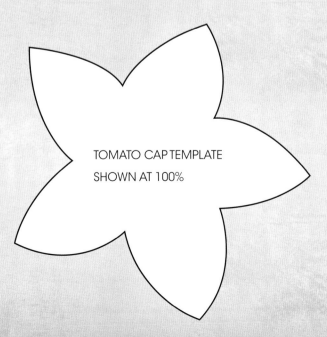

TOMATO CAP TEMPLATE

SHOWN AT 100%

Cabled Pillow Cover
by Cannon-Marie Milby

Update your decor with this elegant cabled pillow cover. The super bulky yarn and tight gauge give the pillow cover fullness and structure.

MATERIALS

2 balls Lion Brand Wool-Ease Thick & Quick Yarn (106 yds/97m) or similar super-bulky weight yarn

Size US 10½ (6.5mm) double-pointed knitting needles

Cable needle

Blunt large eye needle

Three 1¼" (3.2cm) toggle buttons

12" × 16" (30.5cm × 40.6cm) pillow insert

GAUGE

9 sts × 17 rows = 4" (10.2cm) on size US 10½ (6.5mm) needles

1 Knit the pillow using the pattern below.

Cast on 56 sts with 14 sts on each needle. Join yarn to work in the round, being careful not to twist the stitches.

Work in rib (k2, p2) for 6 rnds.

Rnds 1–2: *K4, p4, repeat from * 6 times.
Rnd 3: *Slip 2 sts to a cable needle and hold at back, k2, k2 from cable needle, p4, repeat from * 6 times.
Rnds 4–8: *K4, p4, repeat from * 6 times.
Rnd 9: *Slip 2 sts to a cable needle and hold at back, k2, k2 from cable needle, p4, repeat from * 6 times.

Repeat Rnds 4–9 six times.

Rnds 46–48: *K4, p4, repeat from * 6 times.

Work in rib (k2, p2) for 15 rows, then bind off.

2 Lay the piece flat with the 15 rows of ribbing on the right and the RS (with the cables) inside. With a large eye needle, seam the back to front the left edge.

3 Turn pillow cover right-side out and sew buttons onto the front, right side. Insert pillow form. Fold the back over the buttons and pull the buttons through the back, between the stitches.

Warm and Cozy Tea Cozy
by Doris Lovadina-Lee

Darjeeling, English Breakfast, Yunnan or Assam, whatever you choose, your tea time will be more delightful with this beautiful appliquéd tea cozy.

MATERIALS

8" (20.3cm) square of fusible web

8" (20.3cm) square of cotton print (for appliqué)

Freezer paper

16" × 18" (40.6cm × 45.7cm) piece of cotton fabric (for top)

Two 8" (20.3cm) squares of tear-away stabilizer

16" × 18" (40.6cm × 45.7cm) piece of cotton fabric (for lining)

16" × 18" (40.6cm × 45.7cm) piece of batting

1¼" (3.2cm) × WOF strip (for binding and loop)

Threads to coordinate with fabric appliqué, background and binding

Note
WOF stands for "width of fabric."

1 Fuse the fusible web to the wrong side of the appliqué fabric following the manufacturer's directions. Trim the appliqué to a 7" (17.8cm) square, leaving the paper on the back.

2 Trace the appliqué shape onto freezer paper. Iron the freezer paper onto the right side of appliqué fabric. Let cool. Remove the paper from the fusible web. Carefully cut along the lines of the appliqué (a craft knife works best). You will have a positive and negative shape of the teacup.

3 Take the 16" × 18" (40.6cm × 45.9cm) top fabric and finger press in half (8" × 18" [20.3cm × 45.9cm]), open up and refold 2½" (6.4cm) from the other 2 shorter edges (Figure 1). Finger press.

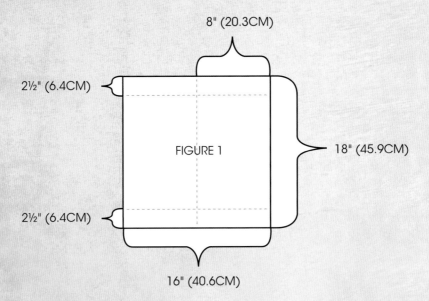

8" (20.3CM)

2½" (6.4CM)

FIGURE 1

18" (45.9CM)

2½" (6.4CM)

16" (40.6CM)

4 Begin with the negative shape (the teacup shape in the square) and position the center line of the appliqué along the line you have just finger pressed. The appliqué square should be 8" (20.3cm) in from the edge and 2½" (6.4cm) from the bottom edge. Once the appliqué is in place, carefully remove the freezer paper and fuse the fabric in place following the manufacturer's directions. (You can lightly press the four corners to help adhere the appliqué to the top, let cool; carefully remove the freezer paper and then fuse.)

5 Take the freezer paper template you have just removed and place it on the opposite side of the top piece. Pin the 4 corners of the paper using the same placement as the front. (The freezer paper is used to help position the positive appliqué shape.)

6 Take the positive appliqué teacup; remove the freezer paper template and place inside the square freezer paper. Once the appliqué teacup is in position, carefully remove the pinned freezer paper and fuse the appliqué shape. (Use a few pins to help hold the teacup shape in place; you can do this on an ironing board and jab the pins straight into the board.)

7 Position 1 square of stabilizer on the wrong side of each of the appliqués. Baste in place. Using a satin stitch on your machine, stitch around each of the appliqué shapes. Remove the stabilizer from the back. Press.

8 Place the lining fabric right-side down; place the batting on top. Place the appliquéd top right-side up on the batting. Baste. Free motion quilt the layers together. (I used a loop all over with a smaller, tighter loop inside the teacup.)

9 Trim the rectangle to 14" × 17½" (35.6cm × 44.5cm). Cut the rectangle in half (14" × 8¾" [35.6cm × 22.2cm]). You now have the front and back of the tea cozy. From the top right corner of the front piece, measure 2½" (6.4cm) across the top and down the side. Mark both measurements with a dot, draw a line connecting the dots and cut along this line. Repeat for the top left side. Do the same for the back of the tea cozy.

10 To make the loop, cut a 4" (10.2cm) piece from your binding strip. Fold ¼" (6mm) in along both sides, press. Fold in half and topstitch the 4" (10.2cm) length closed. Take the 4" (10.2cm) loop piece and fold in half to make a 2" (5.1cm) loop, pin to the top center front of the tea cozy. Stay stitch in place. Place the front and back of the tea cozy right sides together and stitch a ¼" (6mm) seam allowance, leaving the bottom edge free. Press seams open. Serge or zigzag around the raw edges of each piece.

11 Fold over ¼" (6mm) of the 1¼" (3.2cm) wide binding strip and press. Place the unpressed edge of the binding strip to the wrong side of the tea cozy, right sides together, raw edges even. Stitch with a ¼" (6mm) seam allowance. Finger press the binding over the raw edges to the right side of the tea cozy. Make certain that the ¼" (6mm) fold covers the stitching line. Topstitch close to the folded edge.

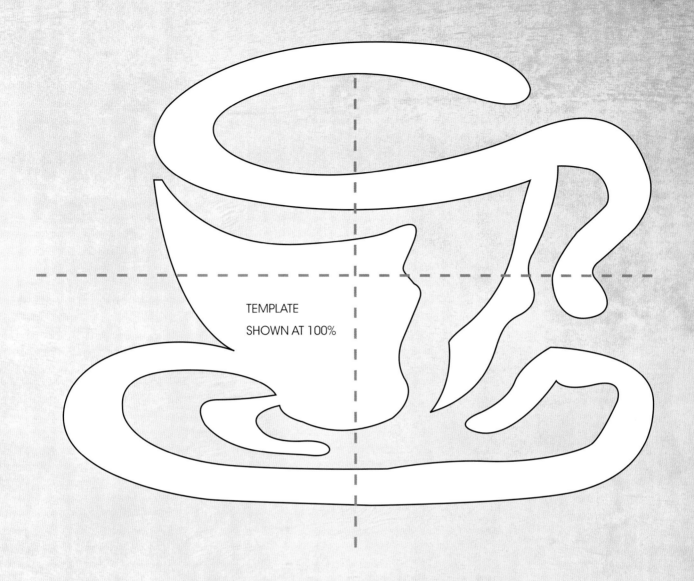

TEMPLATE
SHOWN AT 100%

"Call Me Friend" Card
by Lisa Swift

This is the perfect card to celebrate a special friendship or to say thank you to a friend.

MATERIALS

4" × 5½" (10.2cm × 14cm) white card base

3⅞" × 5⅜" (9.9cm × 13.7cm) red cardstock

Rolling adhesive

2 sheets printed scrapbook paper, striped and floral

1" × 4⅞" (2.5cm × 12.1cm) white scalloped cardstock

White thread

Two 12" (30.5cm) strips of vellum or washi tape

Glue Dots

1 blue die cut paper flower*

1 decorated chipboard coffee mug*

2 sentiment stickers*

1 blue die cut banner*

*Note
I used *Just Because Fresh Verse* stickers; *Just Because Paper Crafting Kit* diecuts (flower, banner); and *Just Because Chipboard* (coffee cup) by Little Yellow Bicycles.

1 Center and glue the red cardstock to the front of the card base.

2 Cut a 3¾" × 5¼" (9.8cm × 13.3cm) piece of striped scrapbook paper. Layer a 2" × 5⅜" (5.1cm × 13.7cm) vertical strip of floral scrapbook onto the striped paper, ¾" (19.1cm) in from the left side of the striped paper. Tuck the white scalloped cardstock behind the left side of the floral paper.

3 With white thread and a sewing machine, stitch straight along the left and right sides of the floral paper, about ⅛" (3mm) in from each edge. Glue to the card.

4 Create a flower embellishment for the front of the card: Glue two ⅝" × 12" (1.6cm × 30.5cm) pieces of vellum tape to white cardstock strips of the same size. Cut the strips into 2" (5.1cm) sections. Roll each section gently around a pencil or dowel to soften the cardstock. Form each strip into a petal shape. Secure each petal with a Glue Dot between the layers.

5 Cut a 2" (5.1cm) circle from white cardstock. Use Glue Dots to adhere the finished petals to the circle, fanning them out to form a flower shape.

6 Embellish the finished flower with a blue die-cut flower, chipboard embellishment, sentiment sticker and banner. Add sentiment stickers to the bottom right corner of the card.

Upcycled Bottles
by Lisa Swift

This fun and easy home decor project showcases a trio of colored bottles decorated with the textures of burlap, canvas and jute.

MATERIALS

3 colored glass bottles, in various heights (the tallest bottle with a cork stopper)

½ yd (45.7cm) burlap fabric

Craft glue

Package of colored jute

Black, brown, red and aqua stamping ink

6 word stamps

3 premade canvas flowers

White cardstock

Fine-tip scissors

2 memo pins

Canvas sentiment sticker

Sentiment sticker, such as "friendship"

Scalloped burlap sticker tag

12" (30.5cm) copper wire

Wire cutters

Felt bird sticker

1 Cut a piece of burlap fabric to fit around the center of each bottle. Glue the fabric around each bottle. When dry, wrap colored jute around the center third of the burlap fabric. Secure the ends with a bit of glue.

2 Use permanent black stamping ink to repeatedly stamp the petals of 3 premade canvas flowers with words. Use brown stamping ink to ink the edges of all flower leaves. Glue the flowers to the front of each bottle.

3 Use stamping ink in black, red and aqua to stamp large words onto a piece of white cardstock. Use fine-tip scissors to cut around the words. and glue the words along the top edge of the burlap on each bottle.

4 For the large bottle: Place a memo pin into the cork at the mouth of the bottle. Add a canvas word sticker between the prongs of the memo pin.

5 For the medium bottle: Tuck a metal memo pin behind the burlap and place a sentiment sticker between the prongs of the memo pin. Glue a scalloped burlap tag to the bottle opening.

6 For the small bottle: Wrap a 12" (30.5cm) length of copper wire around the neck of the bottle. Use wire cutters to cut the wire to desired length. Add a felt bird sticker to the top of the wire.

Hedgehog Frame
by Izzy Anderson

Modify this adorable scene to match the color palette of a baby's nursery or child's room. It's a great way to add a personal touch to home decor.

MATERIALS

8" × 10" (20.3cm × 25.4cm) picture frame

White and coral cardstock

Chipboard pennants*

Patterned paper in a small design (for the kite) and a large design (for the background)

3 buttons

Self-adhesive foam mounts

Twine

Envelope and tag*

Phrase stickers*

*Note
I used paper and embellishments from *Fancy Pants Designs* (the Trend Setter collection).

1 Cut the cardstock to cover the frame base. On top, add a slightly smaller piece of patterned paper and stitch together around the edges using a sewing machine.

2 Add 3 pennants to the upper left of frame and glue in place.

3 Cut a diamond shape from the cardstock and patterned paper to make a kite. Add a button in the center and a long, flowing twine tail.

4 Cut a hedgehog shape from the cardstock. To make the spine, adhere the twine in tight loops along the back side of the hedgehog's back. Cut the loops and add a button embellishment.

5 Use foam adhesive to adhere the hedgehog onto the lower left of the background (this will give the hedgehog some dimension).

6 Layer a tag on top of a patterned envelope. Embellish with phrase stickers and a button. Frame the finished picture.

Purple Bloom Hanging Pocket

by Dian K. Wardhani

The unique combination of felt and patchwork make this wall hanging both beautiful and practical. Use the pockets to organize anything from art supplies to mail.

MATERIALS

Three 6½" (16.5cm) squares of floral cotton fabric

Three 6½" × 4¼" (16.5cm × 10.8cm) pieces of foam lining

Fabric glue

Three 2¾" × 4¼" (7cm × 10.8cm) pieces of felt in coordinating colors

Needle and thread

Thin satin ribbon (for decoration)

3 buttons

Six 6½" (16.5cm) squares of felt in a variety of colors

1" (2.5cm) wide ribbon (for hanging)

1 Place a floral square face down. Layer the foam lining on top, aligning the bottom and side edges. Fold the floral fabric over the top edge of the foam and glue in place. Make 3.

2 Take 1 felt rectangle and lay it on top of the floral rectangle, aligning the right, top and bottom edges. Blanket-stitch around the felt, leaving the top open to form a pocket. Repeat twice more, alternating the pocket placement on one pocket so that it aligns on the left side.

3 Glue a piece of ribbon across each pocket, folding the end around the edge and to the back of the pocket. Sew a button in place to cover the other end of the ribbon.

4 Sew the pocket pieces to 3 of the felt squares: Align the pocket along the bottom edge of the square, and then blanket-stitch around the pocket, leaving the top open. Repeat with remaining 2 pockets.

5 Arrange the 3 remaining felt squares in a vertical line about 1" (2.5cm) apart from each other. Lay your ribbon along the squares, leaving about a 6" (15.2cm) loop at the top. Lay the pocket pieces on top, right sides up, and pin in place. Blanket-stitch completely around the square, securing the ribbon in place and attaching the 2 pieces.

Paint and Stitch Robots
by Courtney Kyle

Make use of your multiple crafting skills by painting and stitching these friendly robots onto canvas.

MATERIALS

Two 8" (20.3cm) square canvases

Paintbrushes

Red, yellow, blue, pink, orange, green and white acrylic paint

Pencil (for tracing design)

Black embroidery floss

Needle (a heavier needle is needed for puncturing the painted canvas)

Small, round sponge or pencil with new eraser (to create dots)

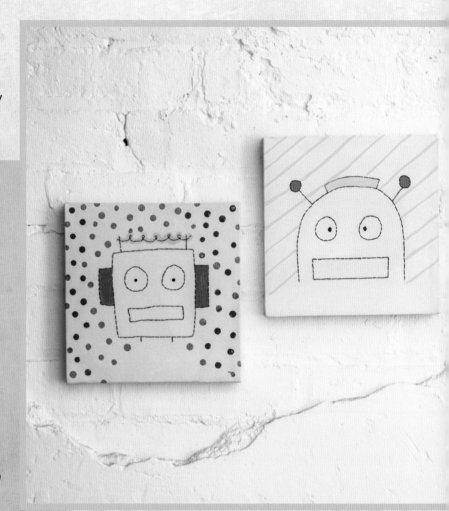

Note

Since canvases are usually framed on wood, be sure to check the back of the canvas to mark a starting point for your robot designs that will be easy for you to stitch. You don't want to try to put your needle down where there is wood!

1 Paint each canvas a solid background color.

2 Lightly trace the robot designs onto the painted canvases using a pencil.

3 Using back-stitch, embroider the robot outlines onto each canvas.

4 Paint around the designs, filling in ears, eyes and antennae as desired. Use the sponge or pencil eraser to paint dots on background as desired.

TEMPLATES

SHOWN AT 100%

Twisted Cowl
by *Beth Major*

This versatile cowl can be twisted and worn around your neck or wrapped around your head. The soft bulky weight yarn works up quickly and easily for instant coziness.

MATERIALS

4 balls Loops & Threads Charisma (109 yds/100m) or similar bulky weight yarn; shown in color Taupe

Size US L (8mm) crochet hook

Stitch marker

GAUGE

9 hdc stitches and 7 rows = 4" (10.2cm)

1 Crochet the cowl using the pattern below.

Create a slip knot leaving approximately a 6" (15.2cm) tail then ch 120. Carefully twist the chain twice then join with sl st to first ch.

Rnd 1: Ch 2, turn, skip the sl st, hdc in first ch (mark this stitch) and in each ch around, join with sl st to first hdc (120 hdc).

Rnd 2: Ch 2, turn, skip the sl st, hdc in first hdc (mark this stitch) and in each hdc around, join with sl st to first hdc (120 hdc).

Repeat rnd 2 for pattern until piece measures approximately 12" (30.5cm) wide. Finish with a complete round then sl st to first hdc in round.

Ch 1, cut the yarn and pull through the last ch stitch. Weave in all the ends, and trim off any excess ends.

Geometric Coaster
by Barbara Swanson

Inspired by Celtic motifs, this coaster is the perfect project to create something special for yourself or for a friend. Change the colors as desired to coordinate with your decor or a special teacup.

*Note
I used Memory Thread colors no. 6380, no. 6390 and no. 6030. For the coordinating thread, I used DMC embroidery floss in colors no. 3834, no. 3812 and no. 613.

MATERIALS

Fabric marker

5" (12.7cm) square of linen

DMC Color Infusions Memory Thread in 3 colors*

Embroidery floss in 3 coordinating colors*

2¾" (7cm) square of light-weight batting

2¾" (7cm) square of cardboard

Craft glue

2⅝" (6.7cm) square of cork

TEMPLATE
SHOWN AT 100%

1 Transfer the template to the center of the linen.

2 Working 1 section of the design at a time, shape and lay the Memory Thread over the pattern, pulling the ends of the Memory Thread through to the back and bending under. Couch the Memory Thread in place using 1 strand of matching floss. Secure the ends of the Memory Thread to the back with a few whip stitches. Repeat this process to complete the design.

3 Layer and adhere batting to the cardboard with the glue.

4 With right side facing up, center the finished piece over the batting and pull the raw edges toward the back of the cardboard. Glue the edges in place.

5 Center and glue the cork to the back.

Full of Flounce Apron
by *Sharon Madsen*

Simply sew five half-circles to a fabric base and voilà! You have a fun and flirty apron perfect for all your kitchen adventures.

MATERIALS

7 coordinating fat quarters*

2¼ yds (2.1m) rickrack

Coordinating thread

*Note

A fat quarter is an 18" × 22" (45.7cm × 55.9cm) piece of fabric, often sold precut at fabric stores.

1 Using the template, cut 3 flounce circles from 1 fat quarter for each apron flounce (5 flounces total). For the apron base cut 1 rectangle 22" × 18" (55.9cm × 45.7cm). Cut 3 rectangles 21" × 3½" (53.3cm × 8.9cm) and 2 rectangles 10½" × 3½" (26.7cm × 8.9cm) for the waistband and ties.

2 With wrong sides together, along the short edges, stitch 3 flounce circles together to create 1 apron flounce, leaving 2 short edges unstitched at the end of the flounce. Repeat for each of the apron flounces. Staystitch ⅜" (1cm) from the top inner curved edge of flounce. Carefully clip curves up to the stitch line. Repeat for each of the apron flounces.

3 Double fold the flounce sides and bottom curved edge ¼" (6mm) toward the wrong side; press, and then stitch. Alternately serge-finish the flounce sides and bottom curved edge.

4 Position the apron body right side up on a large flat surface. Measure 3½" (8.9cm) from the top of the apron. Using a removable fabric marker or chalk, draw a horizontal line parallel with the upper edge. From that line measure 3½" (8.9cm) and draw another horizontal line. Continue until 4 horizontal lines are drawn on the apron body, each 3½" (8.9cm) apart.

5 Hem the apron body: double fold 2 long ends and 1 short end ½" (1.3cm) towards the wrong side; press and then stitch.

6 With the apron body and flounces right side up, align the upper edge of a flounce to the upper edge of the apron body; baste. Position the upper edge of the next flounce over the next horizontal line; baste. Continue until all 5 flounces are basted to the apron body.

7 Position rickrack over the raw edges, excluding the top flounce; pin and then stitch. Remove basting stitches.

8 With right sides together, align one 10½" (26.7cm) tie short edge with one 21" (53.3cm) tie short edge; stitch. Repeat to make the other tie. With right sides together, align 1 tie short edge with one waistband short edge; stitch. Repeat to stitch the remaining tie to the opposite waistband short edge.

9 Designate 1 waistband edge as the upper edge. Position the apron wrong side up on a flat work surface. Position the waistband right side down over the apron, aligning upper edges; pin, and then stitch using a ½" (1.3cm) seam allowance. Press the seam toward the waistband. Fold all remaining raw edges ½" (1.3cm) toward the wrong side; press. With wrong sides together, fold the waistband in half lengthwise, enclosing the apron and waistband raw edge; press, and then pin. Edgestitch the waistband lower and short edges.

Cut along the dotted line

FLOUNCE TEMPLATE

ENLARGE AT 200%

Cut 3 for each flounce

Crocheted Posy Ring
by *Melissa Zbikowski*

Add a little pop to your wardrobe by crocheting one of these adorable posy rings. Simple and sweet, this posy also makes the perfect gift for a best friend, sister or bridesmaid, all in less than an hour.

MATERIALS

1 skein Lily Sugar 'n Cream (120 yds/109m) or similar medium-weight yarn in desired color(s)

Size US G-6 (4mm) crochet hook

Stranded cotton floss to match yarn

Felt scraps to match yarn

Adjustable silver, nickel-free ring base with 8mm pad

Industrial strength glue (such as E-6000 adhesive)

GAUGE

Gauge is not critical to this project.

1 Crochet the flower using the pattern below.

Ch 18.

Row 1: Dc in 3rd ch from hook and each st across (16 dc). Fasten off and weave in ends.

2 Begin winding the crocheted piece into a ball, forming a posy. As you wind the crocheted piece, take an embroidery needle and embroidery floss and stitch a few times in between the wound rows, attaching the rows together. This will help to secure the posy and keep it from unraveling. Once the posy is completely wound, sew the end of the crocheted piece down.

3 Cut a circle out of felt the width of the base of the posy to cover the crocheted back. Whipstitch the felt circle onto the base of the posy using embroidery floss. This will cover the crocheted bottom and hold the posy in place.

4 Glue the felt bottom of the posy onto the ring base. Let the ring dry overnight before wearing.

Broken Jewelry Pendant
by Melissa McLawhorn

Give broken jewelry new life with this pendant. If you don't have any broken jewelry on hand, use jewelry you no longer wear and create your own jewelry fragment.

MATERIALS

- 2" × 2½" (5.1cm × 6.4cm) piece of scrap wood

- Metal file or emory board

- Gold paint

- An assortment of broken jewelry

- Small beads

- Industrial-strength craft glue

- Clear spray enamel

- Silver plated bail

- 18" (45.7cm) silver-plated small ball chain

1 File the edges of the wood base until smooth. The pendant will be resting against your neck; make sure the base isn't rough.

2 Paint the base gold and let it dry.

3 Arrange pieces of broken jewelry and beads on the front of the base.

4 Once the pieces are arranged, glue them in place. Glue 1 piece at a time, waiting about 10 to 15 seconds before gluing down another piece. The glue will set within 10 to 15 seconds, so act quickly if you need to rearrange any of your pieces. Let dry overnight.

5 In a well-ventilated area, spray the front of the pendant with clear enamel. Wait 5 minutes and spray again. Set aside for 1 hour.

6 Sign and date the back of the pendant with permanent marker, then spray the back of the pendant as you did in step 5. Let dry for 1 hour.

7 Glue the bail onto the pendant, and let the glue dry for 1 hour. String the pendant onto the chain.

Simply Stitched Tags
by Kajsa Kinsella

Presentation is everything, and with these stylish gift tags, your gifts will look their best!

MATERIALS

Cardstock

Hole punch

Felt scraps

Inkpads in various colors

Glue stick

Glitter gel pens

String

1 Using the tag template, cut a tag out of cardstock. Punch out hole where indicated.

2 Choose either the house or flower design, and cut the template pieces out of felt.

3 Use the inkpad to dab ink around the edges. Glue the felt pieces in place.

4 Using the gel pens, draw stitched lines around the felt designs.

5 Thread a string through the hole in the tag. Add a message to personalize your tag.

GIFT TAG TEMPLATE

SHOWN AT 100%

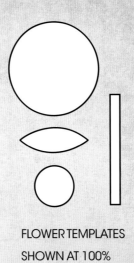

FLOWER TEMPLATES

SHOWN AT 100%

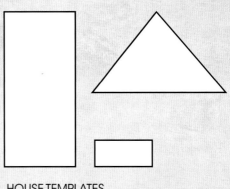

HOUSE TEMPLATES

SHOWN AT 100%

Happy Robot Cross-Stitch
by Courtney Kyle

Bright, happy robots are the focus of this simple cross-stitch, perfect for a baby's room or a quirky wedding gift.

MATERIALS

6" (15.2cm) embroidery hoop

Optional: Acrylic paint

14 count Aida cloth

Embroidery floss in 2 shades of orange, 2 shades of green, magenta and yellow

Craft glue

1 Paint the embroidery hoop, if desired, and let it dry for an hour before hooping the cloth.

2 Follow the cross-stitch chart to stitch the happy robots design. Backstitch where indicated.

3 Trim the excess fabric from the back. Unhoop the cross-stitch and iron the fabric. Add a drop of glue to the hoop and rehoop the cross-stitch.

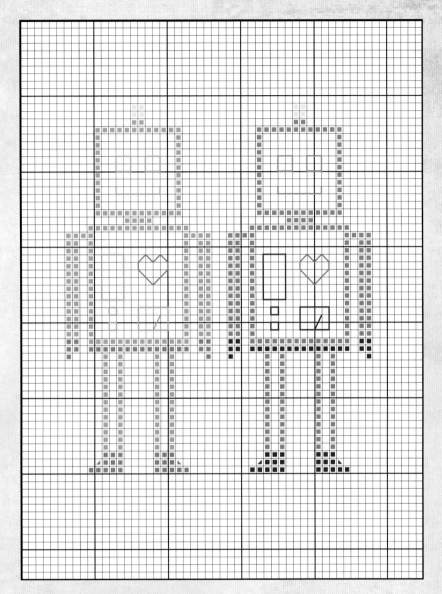

CROSS-STITCH CHART

KEY

▓ Dark Orange
▓ Light Orange
▫ Yellow
■ Light Green
■ Dark Green

——— backstitch
■ cross-stitch
◢ half cross-stitch

Fair Isle Tablet Cover
by Izumi Ouchi

This tablet cover is the perfect size for a standard iPad. The stranded colorwork is from a traditional Estonian mitten pattern, which looks beautiful in contrasting colors.

MATERIALS

Size US 7 (4.5mm) circular needle or a set of double-pointed needle

131 yds (119.8m) each of medium-weight yarn in 3 contrasting colors (navy blue, beige and red)

Stitch marker

Tapestry needle

Size US 6 or 7 (4mm or 4.5mm) crochet hook

1¾" (4.4cm) button

GAUGE

22 sts and 24 rows = 4" (10cm) Adjust needle sizes to obtain the correct gauge.

FINISHED DIMENSIONS

8¾" × 8" (22.2cm × 20.3cm)

COLORWORK CHART

1 Knit the cover using the pattern below.

With circular needle and Main Color (MC), cast on 96 sts, join in the round. Insert a stitch marker to indicate the end of the round. K 1 rnd using MC.

Rnds 2–4: *K2 in MC, p2 in a contrasting color (CC1). Repeat from * to the end of the row.
Rnds 5–7: *K2 in MC, p2 in a second contrasting color (CC2). Repeat from * to the end of the row.

Work Colorwork Chart twice, repeating the 16 sts. Repeat the first 8 rnds once more (40 rnds total), changing to CC2 on Rnd 17 and Rnd 33 instead of CC1.

2 Separate sts onto 2 double-pointed needles (48 sts each needle) and work kitchener stitch in MC using a tapestry needle.

3 Using the crochet hook, work single crochet around cast-on sts to reinforce the opening edge. Sew on button at the top front.

4 Make the button loop: Ch 18 and work 1 row of sc. End off. Fold in half to create a loop and sew the loop opposite the button.

Spiral Wire Earrings
by Lynn Hedgecock

Silver wire twists around Swarovski crystals, giving the illusion of movement in this quick project. Try using different lengths and colors of wire and different beads to change the look of the earrings.

MATERIALS

- 20 gauge wire, such as Parawire
- Wire cutters
- Round nose pliers
- Wooden no. 2 pencil
- Two 3" (7.6cm) headpins
- Eight 3mm silver round beads
- Four 6mm Swarovski bicones
- Two 4mm Swarovski bicones
- Two 5mm jump rings
- 2 ear wires or posts

1 Cut a 4" (10.2cm) piece of wire and, using round nose pliers, form a small loop at one end. Bend the loop so that the long end of the wire is at a right angle to the loop.

2 Hold the loop flat and tight against the side of a pencil with one hand. With the other hand grasp the long end of the wire and wrap the wire around the pencil, keeping the coils tight and close to each other.

3 Slide the wire coil off the pencil, and then, using your fingers, gently pull straight down on the coils, stretching and separating them, creating the outer spiral of the earrings. Set the spiral aside.

4 On 1 of the head pins, string a 3mm round bead, a 6mm crystal bicone, a 3mm round, a 4mm crystal bicone, a 3mm round, a 6mm crystal bicone and a 3mm round. Using the round nose pliers, make a loop near the beads; close the loop by wrapping the wire between the loop you just made and the top 3mm round bead 2 or 3 times (a wire-wrapped loop). Wire wrapping the loop gives it added security. Cut off any excess wire, making sure that the end of the wire is close to the top and not sticking out.

5 Take the beaded headpin, and slide it up the middle of the coiled wire that you previously made so that the loop on top of the headpin and the loop on top of the coiled wire are together. Attach a 5mm jump ring to these 2 loops. To open a jump ring, hold each side of the ring with pliers and push one side away from you while pulling the other side slightly towards you. To close the ring, reverse the push/pull direction.

6 Attach the 5mm jump ring with the coiled wire and beads to an ear wire. Repeat steps 1 through 6 for the second earring.

Upcycled Metal Tin

by *Lisa Swift*

Give old tins new life with a quick makeover. Use your repurposed tin to store buttons, coins or any small items you have around the house.

MATERIALS

- Solid green scrapbook paper or cardstock
- Circle cutter or punch
- Liquid glue
- Tin
- Paper trimmer
- Adhesive canvas tape, twill or ribbon
- Premade flower embellishment
- Craft glue

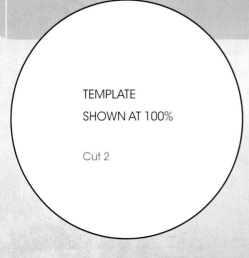

TEMPLATE

SHOWN AT 100%

Cut 2

1 Using the template, cut 2 circles from green scrapbook paper or cardstock. Using liquid glue, adhere 1 circle to the top of the lid and 1 on the underside of the lid.

2 Use a paper trimmer to cut the canvas tape (or adhesive twill or ribbon) into 2 pieces, one ¼" × 9¼" (6mm × 23.5cm) and the other ½" × 9¼" (1.3cm × 23.5cm). Using liquid glue, glue the wider length around the bottom section of the tin and the thinner length around the lid. Trim the tape as needed.

3 Embellish the lid with a premade flower embellishment using craft glue. Let glue dry.

Crochet Butterfly Motif
by Salena Baca

Experiment with different yarn weights to create butterflies in a variety of sizes. These butterflies are great as hairclips, hat and scarf embellishments, and much more!

MATERIALS

About 10 yds (9.1m) of yarn, any weight

Crochet hook to accompany chosen yarn weight

Optional: 1" (2.5cm) alligator clip, hot glue gun and glue sticks

GAUGE

Gauge is not critical to this project.

1 Form an adjustable ring: ch 3, work 2 dc into ring, ch 3 and sl st into ring to connect, (ch 4, work 2 tc into ring, ch 4 and sl st into ring to connect) 2 times, ch 3, work 2 dc into ring, ch 3 and sl st into ring to connect, fasten (16 sts).

2 Tie both tail ends together to fasten, and tuck the ends to the back (the alligator clip will hide the ends).

3 Cut 12" (30.5cm) of a contrasting color yarn. Work a knot at each end (about ¼" [6mm] from end, to keep from fraying). Leaving 2" (5.1cm) free, hold 1 tail end at the top of the butterfly and wrap the yarn around the body twice. Knot both tail ends together (the knot becomes the butterfly's head and the ends are the antennae).

4 Optional: Glue the alligator clip to the back of the butterfly using hot glue.

Carved Clay Bead Necklace
by Niki Meiners

Make a statement with this bold necklace. The beautiful beads are simple to make and look great with everything.

MATERIALS

- White and black polymer clay*
- Pasta machine
- Cookie cutter
- Etching tools
- White paper
- Toothpicks
- Acrylic paint*
- Glazing medium*
- Multipurpose sealer*
- Spring ring clasp
- Silver bead wire
- Silver jump ring

1 Preheat the oven to 250°F (or temperature specified in manufacturer's directions for your specific clay). Condition the clay: Knead manually or pass the clay through a pasta machine several times prior to use. If not well conditioned, your beads may break.

2 Once the clay is conditioned, pass the clay through the pasta machine on the "1" setting. Use a cookie cutter to cut out uniform pieces of clay. For small beads use 1 piece of cut clay. For medium beads stack 2 pieces of clay and for large beads stack 3 pieces. Roll each stack into a ball or whatever shape you choose.

3 Once the beads are formed, use the etching tools to make different patterns in each bead. Use a toothpick to press a hole through the center of each bead. Leave the black beads smooth.

4 To bake beads, make a tray by folding a white piece of paper into an accordion. Place each bead on a toothpick, then place the toothpicks on the folds. Bake the beads for 15 to 30 minutes depending on size. Let cool completely before painting.

5 Mix equal parts of the glazing medium and paint and paint the mixture on the beads. Allow to dry slightly. Use a paper towel to wipe off excess paint and create a worn look. When all the beads are dry, coat them with the multipurpose sealer. Let dry.

6 Place a clasp on the end of the bead wire using pliers. String the beads in desired pattern. Place a jump ring on the other end of the wire.

*Note
I use Sculpey Premo! polymer clay and DecoArt Americana acrylic paint, glazing medium and sealer.

Little Lamb Pin
by Kim Harrington

Wear this adorable felted lamb as a pin or appliqué it onto a
sewing project, hang it as an ornament, use it as an embellishment
on your favorite bag or give as a gift—you can't go wrong!

MATERIALS

White wool roving (for the body)

Felting pad foam or brush (I use a 2" [5.1cm]
thick foam pad)

Felting needles*

Smaller amount of dark roving (for the legs,
eye and nose)

Fine gauge wool yarn (for the collar and tail)

1 tiny bell

Pin back

*Note

Needles often come in a pack
with a red, green and blue tip. The
red tip is the fastest felting needle,
but it is also coarse and leaves
visible holes. The green tip is the
all-purpose needle, and the blue
needle is for delicate work. The
needles are extremely sharp and
barbed, so use with caution.

1 Take a piece of white roving about the size of an egg and shape it into an oval.

Poke the wool onto your felting pad until it is matted together and tightly felted. Felt the wool from both sides. Felt more wool onto the body to get your desired body size. The piece should be about ¼" (6mm) thick.

2 Take a piece of white roving about a third of what you pulled off for the body, and shape the lamb's head, making a roundish triangle. Leave a little of the roving unfelted at the edge where it will attach to the body.

3 Attach the head to the body by poking the unfelted fiber at the edge of the head into the body.

4 Felt a small piece of white roving into a triangle to make the ear. The triangle should be about ¾" (1.9cm). As with the head, leave a small bit of roving at the top of the ear unfelted. Keep turning the piece to felt it from both sides.

5 Attach the ear to the top of the head by poking the fiber into the head and all around the top of the ear. Lift the tip of the ear up and felt underneath it, too, making sure to leave the ear loose at the tip.

6 Make the legs: Roll a small (thumb-size) piece of black roving a into a rectangle. Start poking with your needle and felt into a little flat rectangle the same thickness and firmness as the body. Leave some unfelted wool at the top. Make 2.

7 Place the body about ¾" (1.9cm) over the tops of the legs and felt them into place. Place your needle parallel to the piece and poke the wool at an angle to keep from poking the black wool to the front. Use more white roving to get the legs to stay in place. Turn the piece over and felt from the back, again being careful not to felt through to the front.

8 Form a tiny bit of the dark roving into little balls for the eye and nose. Gently poke them onto the face.

9 String the bell on a piece of fine-gauge wool yarn, and tuck the yarn around the lamb's neck. Tie a knot on the back of the neck, and felt over it with a very thin wisp of roving. Be careful not to catch the yarn on the front of the piece.

10 For the tail, twist a bit of fine gauge wool yarn until it curls back on itself. Poke the raw end of the tail with your needle until it stays twisted on its own.

11 Felt the top of the tail onto the body, leaving the rest of the tail free. If necessary, felt a bit of roving over the tail to help keep it in place.

12 Sew or felt a pin back onto the back of the lamb.

Hidden Pocket Scarf
by Stacy Schlyer

This cozy scarf is more than meets the eye! Under its warm exterior are two hidden pockets, perfect for storing keys, a cell phone and more. Or place hand warmers inside each pocket and keep your hands extra warm.

MATERIALS

¼ yd (22.9cm) fleece fabric

½ yd (45.7cm) fabric (for lining: novelty cotton or flannel work well)*

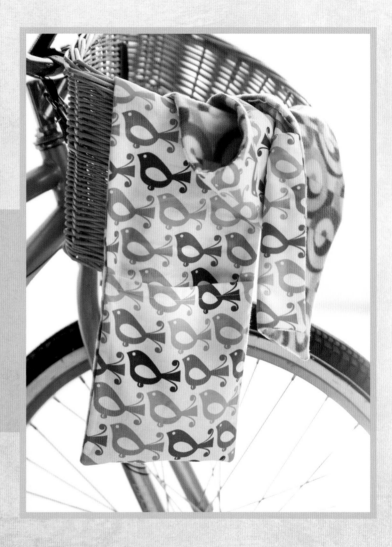

*Note

More material may be needed to match plaids or one-way designs.

All seams are ½" (1.3cm).

1 From the fleece material: Cut one 8" × 57" (20.3cm × 1.5m) rectangle. From the lining material: Cut two 8" × 29" (20.3cm × 73.7cm) rectangles; two 8" × 9½" (20.3cm × 24.1cm) rectangles.

2 Sew together 2 short ends of the 8" × 29" (20.3cm × 73.7cm) lining rectangles, right sides together. Set aside.

3 Fold under ½" (1.3cm) on 1 short edge of a 8" × 9½" (20.3cm × 24.1cm) rectangle to the wrong side of the fabric. Press to crease. Fold again ½" (13cm), press to crease, and stitch in place close to the bottom edge of the fold. Repeat for the second rectangle. These pieces will become the hidden pocket.

4 Place 1 pocket, right-side up, on the right side, bottom edge of the lining. Match the raw edges and baste in place, leaving the finished pocket opening free from stitching. Repeat with the second pocket.

5 Place fleece and lining right sides together, and sew around all sides, leaving a 4" (10.2cm) opening for turning.

6 To reduce bulk at the ends of the scarf, clip the corners of the scarf and turn right-side out. Press the scarf with a cool iron (to keep from melting the fleece material). Hand-stitch the opening closed using a slipstitch.

Colorful Birthday Card

by Benetta Strydom

Use bright, bold, vibrant colors to wish a friend a happy birthday, and bring some color into her life!

MATERIALS

- 6" × 11" (15.2cm × 27.9cm) piece of light yellow marbled cardstock
- Two 2⅜" (6cm) squares of yellow sugar paper
- Two 2⅜" (6cm) squares of orange sugar paper
- Quick-drying glue
- High density sponge
- True red acrylic paint
- Floral paint stamps*
- 25" (63.5cm) of ¼" (6mm) red fabric ribbon
- 4 flowers cut from gold Guipure Lace daisy trim

*Note
I used Jablos Cosmos stamps, PF007.

1 Score the marbled cardstock in half to create a card 6" × 5½" (15.2cm × 14cm).

2 With the fold at the left, glue the yellow sugar paper squares in the bottom left and top right corners, and the orange sugar paper squares in the top left and bottom right corners. To obtain an accurate fit, make light markings on the card where the squares will be glued.

3 Use the sponge to apply an even layer of paint onto the stamp. Transfer the image onto the sugar paper squares by applying even pressure, and then carefully lifting the stamp.

4 Repeat step 3 with the other 2 stamps and allow the stamped images to dry before continuing with the next step.

5 Glue the ribbon around the edges of the sugar paper squares and neatly cut off any protruding edges.

6 Glue the flowers cut from the Guipure Lace trim to the corners of the sugar paper squares.

Sock Yarn Sash
by Kathy North

Self-striping sock yarn creates interesting colorwork bands on this sash belt knit in a seeded rib pattern. Wooden beads and fringe add a touch of 70s hippie style to this fun accessory!

MATERIALS

1 ball Wisdom Yarns Marathon Socks (437 yds/400m) or similar self-striping sock yarn; shown in color Twin Cities

Pair of size US 3 (3.25mm) knitting needles, or size needed to achieve gauge

Crochet hook size US D/3 (3.25mm)

Tapestry needle

8 wooden beads (½" [1.3cm] diameter)

GAUGE

Gauge: 17 sts = 1½" (3.8cm), 9 rows = 1" (2.5cm) in seeded rib pattern on size 3 (3.25mm) needles

1 Knit the sash using the pattern below.

CO 17. Knit 2 rows.

Begin seeded rib pattern:
Row 1 (RS): P1, *k3, p1, rep from * across.
Row 2 (WS): K2, p1, *k3, p1, rep from * to last 2 sts, k2.

Rep Rows 1–2 until piece measures desired length (waist or hip measurement plus 16" [40.6cm] for tying and drop.)

Knit 2 rows and BO.

2 Create the fringe: Wrap yarn around a 6" (15.2cm) measure 20 times. Cut wrap at one end. With crochet hook, attach 2 strands of fringe in each stitch evenly across the cast on/bound off stitches at each end of the sash. Add the wooden beads by threading 2 strands from each set of adjoining fringes through beads with the tapestry needle and tying overhand knots to hold beads in place. Stagger the placement of 4 beads at each end of the sash as shown.

Fabric Scrap Wreath
by Courtney Kyle

Colorful and reminscent of springtime, this wreath is created using scraps of vintage fabric, colorful buttons and felt flower rosettes.

MATERIALS

Fabric scraps, preferably something that can be torn into strips

10" (25.4cm) diameter wreath, preferably a straw wreath still wrapped in plastic

Fabric glue

Felt

Assorted buttons

1 Using scissors, snip the fabric along the edge every 1" to 1½" (2.5cm to 3.8cm), and tear strips. Make sure strips are at least 10" (25.4cm) long to wrap at least once around the girth of the wreath.

2 Wrap strips around the wreath, covering the wreath completely. Glue the ends of the fabric strips down to secure.

3 Create the felt rosettes: Cut circles out of the felt, then cut a spiral into the circle, working your way to the center. (See the template for the Felt Flower Wreath, page 19.) From the outer edge of spiral strip, tightly roll the strip until the end; glue the end of the strip to the bottom of the rosette to secure.

4 Glue rosettes onto wreath. Add buttons, stacking and arranging them around the rosettes. Glue the buttons in place.

Mama and Baby Ladybug Wall Art
by Tara Cousins

This cute little trio of ladybugs will look perfect in any child's room. Made entirely with single crochet, the simplest of crochet stitches, this project can be finished in no time at all.

MATERIALS

50 yds (45.7m) red medium-weight yarn

Size US I (5.5mm) crochet hook

30 yds (27.4m) black medium-weight yarn

GAUGE

Gauge is not critical to this project.

1 Crochet the mama ladybug body using the pattern below.

With red, ch 21.
Row 1: Sc into 2nd ch from hook and each ch across (20 sts).
Rows 2–5: Sc in each st across (20 sts).
Row 6: Sc dec, 16 sc, sc dec (18 sts).
Row 7: Sc in each st across (18 sts).
Row 8: Sc dec, 14 sc, sc dec (16 sts).
Row 9: Sc dec, 12 sc, sc dec (14 sts).
Row 10: Sc dec, 10 sc, sc dec (12 sts).
Row 11: Sc dec, sc dec, 4 sc, sc dec, sc dec (8 sts).

Tie off, weave in loose ends.

2 Crochet the baby ladybugs' bodies (make 2). With red, ch 13.
Row 1: Sc into 2nd ch from hook and each ch across (12 sts).
Rows 2–4: Sc in each st across (12 sts).
Row 5: Sc dec, 8 sc, sc dec (10 sts).
Row 6: Sc dec, 6 sc, sc dec (8 sts).
Row 7: 4 sc dec (4 sts).

Tie off, and weave in loose ends.

3 Crochet the mama ladybug's head and legs. Connect black to bottom corner of mama ladybug body. Work 1 sc.

Form leg: Ch 3, 2 sc back along ch. Continue with 9 sc along bottom of ladybug, ch3, 2 sc back along ch, 9 sc, ch3, 2 sc back along ch, sc in next st (this should be the bottom corner st).

Begin head: Ch 3, 2 sc back along ch. Sl st to red body. ch 1, turn.

Working back along black head: sc, sc inc. Ch 1, turn.

Working back along head again: 3 sc, sl st to next stitch on red body, ch 1, turn. 3 sc, ch 1, turn. Sc dec, sc, sl st to red body. Sc around red body, spacing stitches evenly so ladybug lies flat. Once round is complete, sl st to first sc in round. Tie off.

4 Crochet the baby ladybugs' heads and legs. Connect black to bottom corner of baby ladybug body. Work 1 sc.

Form leg: Ch 2, sc back along ch, sl st to ladybug body in current st.

Continue with 5 sc along bottom of ladybug. Ch 2, sc back along ch, sl st to ladybug body in current st. 5 sc, ch 2, sc back along ch, sl st to ladybug body in current st, sc in next st.

Begin head: Ch 3, 2 sc back along ch. Sl st to red body. ch 1, turn.

Working back along black head: 2 sc. Ch 1, turn.

Working back along head again: sc dec, sl st to next stitch on red body. Sc around ladybug body, spacing stitches evenly so ladybug lies flat. Once round is complete, sl st to first sc in round. Tie off.

5 Make the ladybug spots.

Mama spots (make 3): With black, ch 4. Sl st to first ch to form a loop. Work 7 sc into center of ring. Sl st to first st in round. Tie off, leaving a long tail to sew spot onto ladybug.

Baby spots (make 6): With black, ch 4. Sl st to first ch to form a loop. Tie off, leaving a long tail.

Position spots on ladybugs according to photo. Sew on spots using yarn tail and yarn needle. Weave in the ends.

6 Hang ladybugs on wall using small finishing nails.

Clay Buttons
by Christine Lehto

Try making your own clay imprinting tools to use on these versatile clay buttons. Little flower-shaped gems or embellishments make interesting imprints.

MATERIALS

Polymer clay in color(s) of your choice

Assorted clay tools to imprint into the clay

Needle clay tool

Acrylic paint in colors of your choice

Glaze, preferably Varathane Polyurethane

Optional: magnets, pin backs, jewelry bails

Superglue

Note
You can also make the holes after the clay is baked by using a small drill bit.

1 Preheat your oven according to the baking directions for your clay. Roll a ball of clay approximately ¾" (1.9cm) diameter. Make the ball larger or smaller depending on how large of a button you would like. Press down on the ball of clay to flatten it into a circle shape.

2 Use store-bought or homemade clay tools to press shapes and designs into the circle-shaped clay. If you have some favorite buttons, you can use those to imprint a design into the clay. To make a circular ring indentation within the button, use an item like the plastic cap of a shampoo bottle or soda bottle.

3 Use a needle tool to make button holes in the center of the piece.

4 Once the button is designed to your taste, follow the baking directions on the packaging. Allow the buttons to cool.

5 Paint highlight sections on the button. Let dry. Apply glaze to the surface of the button and let dry.

6 Use superglue to add a magnet, pin back or jewelry bail to the back of the button. You can also use the handmade buttons as decorative embellishments for other projects, such as scrapbook pages, picture frames, etc.

Stitched Circles Pillow

by Melony Miller-Bradley

A great project for using up felt and fabric scraps, this pillow will add style to any room.

MATERIALS

Fabric scraps in coordinating colors and patterns

Fusible webbing

Felt scraps in yellow, turquoise, tan and orange

1 yd (91.4cm) felt

Flat backed buttons (approx. 36)

14" × 12" (35.6cm × 30.5cm) pillow form

1 Fuse webbing to fabric according to manufacturer's directions.

2 Cut 36 circles out of the felt scraps, 2¾" (7cm), 2½" (6.4cm) and 2" (5.1cm) in diameter.

3 Cut 36 circles out of the fabric scraps to fit inside the felt circles, about ¼" (6mm) smaller in diameter.

4 Peel the paper backing away from the fabric circles and fuse them onto the felt circles following the manufacturer's directions.

5 Using a sewing machine, free-form stitch around the circles. Use the various stitches available on your machine, or alternate between straight and zigzag stitch.

6 Cut two 15" × 13" (38.1cm × 33cm) rectangles from the felt. Using a needle and thread, sew a button to the center of each circle. Before knotting the thread in back, sew the circle onto one of the felt rectangles. Continue until all circles have been sewn to pillow front, leaving 1" (2.5cm) around all 4 sides without circles.

7 Place right sides of pillow cover together. Leaving a ½" (1.3cm) seam allowance, sew right, top and left sides of the pillow cover together, leaving bottom open for turning. Steam seams open and insert pillow form. Hand sew the bottom of pillow cover closed with a whipstitch.

Quilted Thank You Note
by Izzy Anderson

Using coordinating paper scraps and a sewing machine, you can create a sweet, inexpensive and thoughtful card, perfect for expressing simple thanks.

MATERIALS

Cardstock

Ribbon

Twine

Square punch

Paper tag*

Patterned paper scraps*

Flower sticker*

Flat backed pearl

Craft glue

*Note
I used paper and stickers from Simple Stories.

1 Use the cardstock to make the card base in your desired dimensions.

2 Make a separate card front, slightly smaller than the card base, in a contrasting cardstock color. Add ribbon and twine on the left side.

3 Punch 16 small squares of patterned paper. Arrange them on the front of the card in a quilt block pattern (you may have to trim some of the squares to fit). Sew in place using a sewing machine.

4 Print a message on the paper tag, either handwritten or using a computer.

5 Punch three small squares of patterned paper and stitch them to the tag. Add ribbon and a small flower sticker with a pearl center.

6 Adhere the tag to the card front.

Two-Round Flower
by Janet Brani

Super easy and super fast, this crocheted flower only takes two rounds to complete. Use it to embellish hats, note cards and scarves.

MATERIALS

2 yds (1.8m) medium-weight yarn (for center)

5 yds (4.6m) medium-weight yarn (for petals)

Small amount of contrasting yarn (for center knots)

Size US G (4mm) or 7 (4.5mm) crochet hook

DIMENSIONS

3" (7.6cm) diameter

GAUGE

Gauge is not critical to this project.

1 Crochet the flower using the pattern below.

Rnd 1: With center color, ch 4, make 13 dc in 4th ch from hook. Sl st top of beginning ch 4. Fasten off.
Rnd 2: Attach the petal color in the space between any 2 stitches on Rnd 1, ch 1, [1 sc, 1 hdc, 1 dc, 1 tr, 1 dc, 1 hdc, 1 sc] in same space. Skip next 2 sts, repeat the stitch sequence in brackets, working between 2 stitches. Repeat for a total of 7 petals, join with sl st to first sc made, fasten off.

2 To close the center hole, thread beginning yarn tail onto a darning needle, run under dc sts and cinch tight. Weave in the end.

3 With contrasting color, make 3 French knots on the flower center.

Very Necessary Needle Book
by Kajsa Kinsella

Make your very own needle book! With just a few simple steps, you will have a trusted sewing companion for years to come.

MATERIALS

3 sheets of colored felt

White cotton fabric

Decorative rubber stamp

Inkpad

Wooden button

1 Cut the first sheet of felt into a 5½" × 4¼" (14cm × 10.8cm) rectangle. Using pinking shears, cut a second rectangle from the second color, slightly smaller than the first, then a third rectangle slightly smaller than the second. Cut the cotton into a 2½" × 3" (6.4cm × 7.6cm) rectangle.

2 Fray the edges of the cotton rectangle by pulling out a few strands along each edge. Decorate the cotton patch using a rubber stamp and ink.

3 Fold the largest rectangle in half, and center the cotton patch on the front half. Unfold and sew the patch in place, going around the edges and diagonally, from corner to corner. Sew the button onto the center of the patch.

4 Lay the felt cover flat, right side down, and then layer in the pages, the larger one first. Fold the book shut to check that the pages are placed correctly.

5 Sew a single seam down the middle of the book attaching the pages to the cover.

Lace Napkin Ring
by Kathy North

An easy-to-knit lace strip is turned into a napkin ring with the addition of crocheted loop edging and two decorative buttons!

MATERIALS

10 yds (9.1m) Patons Grace or similar light-weight cotton yarn

Pair of size US 3 (3.25mm) knitting needles, or size needed to achieve gauge

Crochet hook size US D/3 (3.25 mm)

2 buttons (½" to ⅝" [1.3cm to 1.6cm] diameter)

GAUGE

5 sts and 10 rows = 1" (2.5cm) in garter stitch on size 3 (3.25mm) needles

1 Knit the napkin ring using the pattern below.

Cast on 11 sts. Knit 4 rows in garter stitch.

Begin lace pattern:
Row 1: K1, *k1, yo, sl 1, k2tog, psso, yo, rep from * to last 2 sts, k2.
Rows 2–4: Knit.

Repeat rows 1–4 until piece measures 4½" (11.4cm). BO and weave in ends.

2 Crochet the edging and button loops.

Row 1: With RS facing, attach yarn with crochet hook to first st on cast-on edge of piece. Ch 1, work 10 sc evenly across cast-on sts, turn.
Row 2: Ch 1, sc in each of first 2 sc, *ch 5, sk next 2 sc, sc in each of next 2 sc, rep from * once. Fasten off and weave in ends.

3 With sewing needle and thread, attach buttons to opposite end of piece in line with button loops. Form napkin ring by securing buttons through button loops.

Chunky Mesh Cowl
by Salena Baca

The bulky yarn works up quickly, so you can make several cowls to match your wardrobe, or create a stash just for gift giving! This cowl is made in one piece with a twist so you can wear this as a hood, too!

MATERIALS

2 balls Lion Brand Homespun (186 yds/169m) or similar bulky weight yarn

Size US K (6.5mm) crochet hook

GAUGE

13 sts and 4 rows = 4" (10.2cm) in double crochet on size US K (6.5mm) crochet hook

1 Crochet the cowl using the pattern below.

Ch 50.

Rnd 1: Dc into the 5th ch from hook, (ch 1, skip 1 st, dc into following st) across (24 dc; 47 sts total).

Rnds 2–57: Ch 2 (first dc), turn work, (ch 1, skip 1 st, dc into following st) across (24 dc; 47 sts total).

2 Assemble the cowl: Fold the garment in half lengthwise, turn corners of last row worked so that left corner is on right side, and right corner is on left side; this will add one twist to the garment, and allow you to fasten it together into a tube. Hold first row together with last row worked. Using the BLO of your first and last rows worked, sl st together evenly.

3 Crochet the edging: Work 1 sc into each dc end row around side of garment.

Cut yarn when beginning tail is reached, and weave in the ends (114 sc).

Felt Circles Garland

by Shannon Miller

This sweet decorative garland will add a festive touch to any occasion. Experiment with color and shapes to tailor the garland to your home.

MATERIALS

Wool felt scraps

¼" (6mm)-wide grosgrain ribbon

Note

Use a die-cutting machine and a 1" (2.5cm) circle die for faster, easier cutting!

1 Cut thirty 1" (2.5cm) circles from felt. The sample shown uses 6 circles each of 6 different colors including white, light gray and dark gray along with light, medium and dark yellow.

2 Use a sewing machine to chain-sew all circles together down centers, backstitching on the first and last circles to secure.

3 Cut two 5" (12.7cm) lengths of ribbon. Fold each in half and stitch onto back of last circle on each end, backstitching to secure.

Glam Glass Pearl Necklace
by Vicki Riggan

This necklace is perfect for a bride or for anyone looking to add a touch of glam to their jewelry wardrobe. Quick and easy, this project is suitable for all skill levels.

MATERIALS

Beading wire, such as Soft Flex

14mm pearl focal bead

2 bead caps

Thirty 3mm silver round beads

2 crystal rondells

Two 12mm pearls

Two 6mm crystal bicones

8 silver curved tube beads

Fourteen 6mm pearls

2 silver crimp beads

Jump ring

Spring ring clasp

1 Cut a 22" (55.9cm) length of wire. Starting from the center and working to the left, string a 14mm pearl focal bead, a silver bead cap, a round silver bead, a crystal rondell, a round silver bead, a 12mm pearl, a round silver bead, a crystal bicone bead and a round silver bead. Repeat on the right side. The center section of the necklace is now complete.

2 Working from the left, string *a silver curved bead, a silver round bead, a 6mm pearl, a silver round bead, a 6mm pearl and a silver round bead. Repeat from * twice. End by adding an additional silver curved bead, a round silver bead, a 6mm pearl and a round silver bead. Repeat this sequence on the right side of necklace.

3 To the left side of the necklace, add a crimp bead and jump ring to end of the strand. Thread the wire back through the crimp bead, catching the jump ring and continuing through the first couple of beads at the end of the strand. Pull tight and crimp the bead with crimping tool. Snip off excess wire.

4 To the right side of the necklace, add the crimp bead and spring ring clasp to the end of the strand. Thread the wire back through the crimp bead, catching the loop at the bottom of the spring ring clasp. Thread wire through the first couple of beads at the end of the strand. Pull tight until there are no gaps between beads. Crimp the bead and snip off excess wire.

Glam Glass Pearl Bracelet
by Vicki Riggan

This bracelet pairs perfectly with the *Glam Glass Pearl Necklace*. The directions given are for a 7½"(19.1cm) bracelet. More or fewer beads can be added to adjust the size.

MATERIALS

Beading wire, such as Soft Flex

Sixteen 2mm silver round beads

6 crystal bicone beads

10 silver bead caps

Five 12mm pearls

Four 6mm pearls

Tube-shaped crimp beads

Silver toggle clasp

1 Cut a 10" (22.54cm) piece of wire. You may want to attach a clip on one end of the wire to prevent the beads from sliding off as you string.

2 String the center beads as follows: a silver bead cap, 12mm pearl and a silver bead cap.

3 Working from the left side, string *a silver bead, a crystal bicone, a silver bead, a 6mm pearl, a silver bead, a silver bead cap, a 12mm pearl and a silver bead cap. Repeat from * once. To finish the left side, add a silver bead, a crystal bicone and a silver bead.

4 Repeat step 3 on the right side of the bracelet. If making a 7½" (19.1cm) bracelet, you should now have five 12mm pearls, four 6mm pearls and 6 crystal bicone beads on the strand.

5 To finish, thread a crimp bead and the toggle bar onto the strand. Thread wire back through crimp bead and push wire through the first several beads on strand. Crimp bead using a crimping tool or pliers. Trim excess wire.

6 Repeat step 4 on the right side of the strand. Before you do the final crimp, pull wire tight enough that all the beads on the strand are snug against each other and no gaps remain between the beads. Crimp and trim excess wire.

Owl Crayon Case
by Anastasia & Marina Popova

Send your little one off to school with their own special crayon case. Made from felt, it's a quick and a fun project to make.

MATERIALS

White, gray, orange, blue and yellow felt

Fabric glue

2 buttons

1 Use the templates to cut out the felt.

2 Using the photo as a guide for placement, glue the paws to the body and the eyes to the face.

3 Glue the face to the body and hand sew around it to secure the face in place, especially the points. Use small and evenly spaced stitches.

4 Sew the buttons on over the felt eyes.

5 Sew the body pieces together using a blanket stitch. Leave the bottom open.

FACE TEMPLATE

SHOWN AT 100%

Cut 1 from gray felt

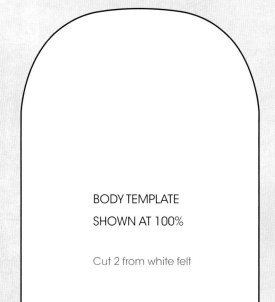

BODY TEMPLATE

SHOWN AT 100%

Cut 2 from white felt

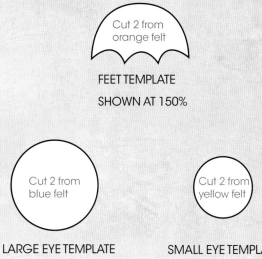

Cut 2 from orange felt

FEET TEMPLATE

SHOWN AT 150%

Cut 2 from blue felt

Cut 2 from yellow felt

LARGE EYE TEMPLATE

SHOWN AT 150%

SMALL EYE TEMPLATE

SHOWN AT 150%

Felt Flower Barrette

by Barbara Swanson

The wire in the Memory Thread adds shape and dimension to this barrette. Make an extra flower to accent a hat band or create one for special occasions using white felt and silver or gold thread.

MATERIALS

Blue, green and neon green felt

DMC Color Infusions Memory Thread in 5 colors*

Embroidery floss in 4 coordinating colors*

Craft glue

One 4" (10.2cm) spring clip barrette

1 Cut the felt shapes as directed on the templates.

2 Shape the turquoise Memory Thread as directed on the small flower pattern , crimping under ¼" (6mm) of each end for a smooth finish. Couch the turquoise Memory Thread in place using 1 strand of coordinating floss. Repeat this process for the remaining petals.

3 Repeat step 2 to complete the leaves, using light green Memory Thread on the neon green felt and dark green Memory Thread on the green felt.

4 Twist the yellow and orange Memory Thread together to create one length and coil it into a small spiral, approximately ½" (1.3cm) in diameter. Crimp the ends under and couch the spiral to the center of the small flower shape using 1 strand of floss.

5 Layer the completed petal and leaf shapes as shown and glue to secure.

6 Glue the completed flower to the barrette. Let dry completely before wearing.

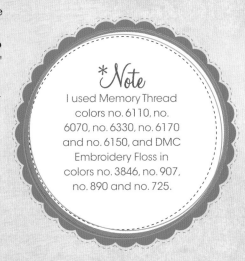

*Note
I used Memory Thread colors no. 6110, no. 6070, no. 6330, no. 6170 and no. 6150, and DMC Embroidery Floss in colors no. 3846, no. 907, no. 890 and no. 725.

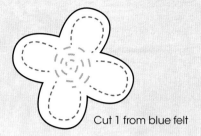

Cut 1 from blue felt

MIDDLE PETAL TEMPLATE

SHOWN AT 100%

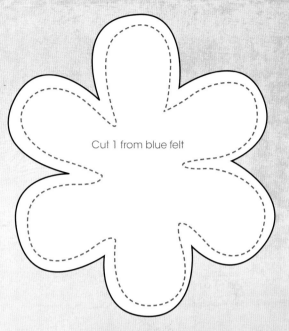

Cut 1 from blue felt

Cut 1 from blue felt

OUTER PETAL TEMPLATE

SHOWN AT 100%

INNER PETAL TEMPLATE

SHOWN AT 100%

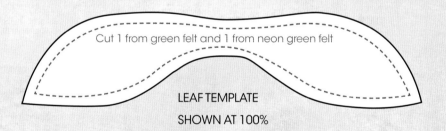

Cut 1 from green felt and 1 from neon green felt

LEAF TEMPLATE

SHOWN AT 100%

Note
Solid lines are for cutting,
dashed lines are for
Memory Thread placement.

Tea Bag Holder
by Sheryl Hastings

This little case can be used for numerous things! They are perfect for presenting a gift card, or storing your own gift or credit cards. I'm a tea lover so that's my favorite way to use them.

MATERIALS

Scrap cardstock

Small scraps of paperbacked fusible webbing

Smaller felt scraps (for teapot and teacup)

Medium weight fusible interfacing

4¾" × 6¾" (12.1cm × 17.1cm) piece of felt

Embroidery floss

Mini button (6mm) or bead

Two 1¼" × 2½" (3.2cm × 6.4cm) pieces of felt (for closure)

¾" (1.9cm) button

¾" (1.9cm) square piece of hook and loop fastener

Thick and tacky craft glue

FINISHED DIMENSIONS

3¼" × 4¾" (8.3cm × 12.1cm)

1 Copy the templates onto cardstock. With the printed side of the templates facedown, trace around the templates onto the paper side of your paperbacked fusible webbing. Fuse these pieces onto the felt scraps you have chosen for your appliqués. Cut out and remove the paper backing. Be sure to follow the manufacturer's directions for the fusible webbing you will be using. Set aside.

2 Fuse the fusible interfacing to the larger piece of felt, following the manufacturer's directions. Trim the edges of the interfacing just a smidge so that none of the interfacing will peek through when you are finished.

3 Place the large piece of felt with the interfacing side facing down on an ironing board, portrait style. Find the center point between the upper half and the lower half. This is your fold line. Lay a piece of paper or pencil there so you know where the fold will be. Arrange the appliqués on the upper half of the felt. Make sure that the appliqués are at least ¼" (6mm) away from each edge and the fold line. (See photo for placement.) Fuse all pieces in place.

4 Stitch around the appliqué pieces using 3 strands floss and a blanket stitch. Use 3 strands of floss and backstitches to make the steam from the cup. For the cup handle, use 6 strands of floss and backstitches. Stitch the mini button or bead onto the top of the teapot.

5 Round the corners on one end of each felt closure piece. Layer the closure pieces together and blanket-stitch around them using 3 strands of floss. Stitch the button on the edge with rounded corners.

6 Stitch each short edge of the large felt appliquéd piece using 3 strands and a blanket stitch. Fold in half with wrong sides together and blanket-stitch up each side with 3 strands.

7 Glue 1 piece of the hook and loop tape on the underside of the closure. Glue the remaining piece at the center of the front, close to the upper edge. Let the glue dry completely, then close the hook and loop tape. Bring the other end of the closure to the back of the case and glue in place. Let dry before using.

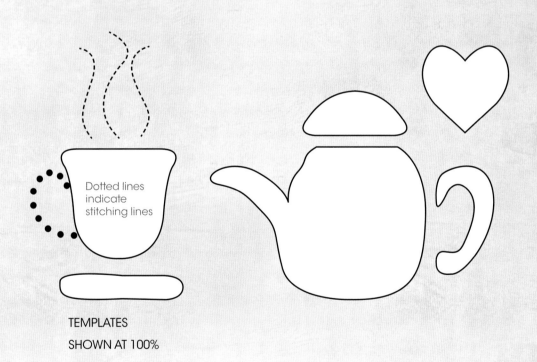

Dotted lines indicate stitching lines

TEMPLATES

SHOWN AT 100%

Monogram Frame
by Lisa Swift

Great as a wedding gift or for a nursery, this framed monogram makes use of premade embellishments so it's easy and fun to assemble.

MATERIALS

Piece of thin cardboard or chipboard

Piece of burlap fabric

Craft glue

5" × 7" (12.7cm × 17.8cm) wood frame

6" (15.2cm) wood monogram

Black spray paint

Sandpaper

Glue Dots

3 premade canvas flowers

Printed canvas tape

Stick pin with wood topper

Scalloped canvas sentiment sticker

Printed canvas word, such as "family"

Brown and black stamping ink

3D foam squares

Word stamp, such as "cherish"

Sheet of vellum paper

1 Cut a 5" × 7" (12.7cm × 17.8cm) piece of cardboard or chipboard and cut a 5" × 7" (12.7cm × 17.8cm) piece of burlap fabric. Glue the burlap to the cardboard or chipboard. When dry, insert this piece into the frame, under the glass.

2 Spray paint the wood monogram black. When dry, sand the edges and adhere the monogram to the outside center of the glass with Glue Dots.

3 Embellish the top and bottom areas of the frame, as well as the monogram, with premade canvas, burlap and wood embellishments. Use brown ink to ink the edges of the flower leaves before adhering. Use 3D foam squares to give the canvas tape banners and scalloped canvas sticker some dimension and lift.

4 Stamp a sentiment in black ink onto a 2½" × ½" (6.4cm × 1.3cm) piece of vellum. Use scissors to notch both ends into a banner shape and adhere this piece over the canvas word at the bottom of the frame.

Zebra Cowl
by Kathy North

This cowl has a stylish "zebra" look and an interesting texture created by working two colors in alternate rounds of back loop only crochet.

MATERIALS

1 ball Classic Elite "Wool Bam Boo" (118 yd/107.9m) or similar fine or light-weight yarn, in white

1 ball Classic Elite "Wool Bam Boo" (118 yd/107.9m) or similar fine or light-weight yarn, in black

Crochet hook size US H/8 (5mm), or size needed to achieve gauge

Tapestry needle

GAUGE

13 sts and 8 rows = 4" (10.2cm) in dc on size US H/8 (5mm) hook

1 Crochet the cowl using the pattern below.

With black, ch 91, join into ring, being careful not to twist ch.

Rnd 1: Ch 1, sc in first ch, hdc in each of next 2 ch, dc in each of next 4 ch, hdc in each of next 2 ch, sc in next ch, *sc in next ch, hdc in each of next 2 ch, dc in each of next 4 ch, hdc in each of next 2 ch, sc in next ch, rep from * around, join with sl st to beg sc, drawing the white through at last step (90 sts). Drop the black, but do not cut it.

Rnd 2: Working in blo on this and all following rnds, with white, ch 1, sc in same sc, hdc in each of next 2 hdc, dc in each of next 4 dc, hdc in each of next 2 hdc, sc in next sc, *sc in next sc, hdc in each of next 2 hdc, dc in each of next 4 dc, hdc in each of next 2 hdc, sc in next sc, rep from * around, join with sl st, drawing the black through at last step. Drop the white but do not cut it.

Rnd 3: Cont to work in blo, with the black, ch 1, sc in same sc, hdc in each of next 2 hdc, dc in each of next 4 dc, hdc in each of next 2 hdc, sc in next sc, *sc in next sc, hdc in each of next 2 hdc, dc in each of next 4 dc, hdc in each of next 2 hdc, sc in next sc, rep from * around, join with sl st, drawing the white through at last step. Drop the black but do not cut it.

Rnds 4–9: Rep rnds 2–3. At the end of rnd 9, fasten off and weave in the ends.

Framed Ornaments
by *Izzy Anderson*

Use chipboard frames in nontraditional colors to create homemade ornaments. These ornaments are very light and won't weigh down your tree branches.

MATERIALS

Colorful chipboard frames*

Craft glue

Patterned paper scraps*

Alphabet stickers*

Small chipboard stickers*

Flat backed pearls and gems

Twine

Snowflake punch

Ribbon pieces

Note
I used paper and embellishments from Fancy Pants Designs (the Trend Setter collection).

1 Assemble the small chipboard frames. For each, layer a thin frame on top of a larger decorative frame. This adds dimension and color to the ornaments. If you don't have premade frames, you can make your own using plain chipboard, covering them with acrylic paint, patterned paper or decorations of your choice. The frames can be as simple or ornate as you like.

2 Back each frame with colorful patterned paper. Small prints work best. To make the ornaments stand out on the tree, choose nontraditional colors and patterns.

3 Use letter stickers to add short sentiments to each frame, and decorate as desired.

4 Add ribbon hangers to the back of each frame.

Square Cabled Pillow Cover
by Cannon-Marie Milby

This pillow cover features an envelope back with button closures. The super bulky yarn gives the pillow cover a nice full feel.

MATERIALS

2 balls Lion Brand Wool-Ease Thick & Quick Yarn (106 yds/97m) or similar super bulky weight yarn

Size US 13 (9mm) knitting needles

Cable needle

Four 1¼" (3.2cm) buttons

16" (40.6cm) square pillow insert

GAUGE

9 stitches × 12 rows = 4" (10.2cm) on US 13 (9mm) needles

1 Knit the pillow using the pattern below.

Back

Cast on 18 sts for back piece A and work in St st (k on RS, p on WS) until the piece measures about 16" (40.6cm) from cast-on edge. Bind off.

Cast on 18 sts for back piece B and work in St st (k on RS, p on WS) until the piece measures about 16" (40.6cm) from cast-on edge. Pick up 24 sts in "chain" along the left side of back piece B. Knit in rib (p2, k2) for 6 rows. Bind off.

Front
Cast on 36 sts.
Row 1: K12, p3, k6, p3, k12
Row 2: P12, k3, p6, k3, p12

Repeat rows 1–2 four times.
Row 11: K12, p3, slip next 3 sts to a cable needle and hold at back, k3, k3 from cable needle, p3, k12
Repeat rows 1–11 twice.

Row 34: K12, p3, k6, p3, k12
Row 35: P12, k3, p6, k3, p12

Repeat rows 34–35 four times. Bind off.

2 Lay the front piece on a flat surface with RS facing up. Lay back piece A on the front piece with RS facing down and left, top and bottom edges of the 2 pieces aligned. Seam back piece A to the front, sewing around the bottom, left and top edges.

3 Lay back piece B, right side down, on top of the front piece and overlapping back piece A. Align the right, top and bottom edges. Seam the edges together, leaving the ribbed edge free.

4 Turn the pillow cover right-side out and sew the buttons along the edge of back piece A. Insert pillow form. Pull back piece B over the buttons and pull the buttons through the ribbing.

Anchor Cross-Stitch
by Courtney Kyle

This simple cross-stitch features a bold red anchor framed by a navy blue embroidery hoop.

MATERIALS

5" (12.5 cm) embroidery hoop

Navy blue acrylic paint

Paintbrush

14-count Aida cloth

Red embroidery floss

Craft glue

1 Paint the embroidery hoop, and let it dry for an hour before hooping the cloth.

2 Follow the cross-stitch chart to stitch the anchor design.

3 Trim the excess fabric from the back. Unhoop the design, and iron it. Apply a bead of glue to the hoop before rehooping the cross-stitch.

CROSS-STITCH CHART

KEY

■ cross-stitch
◢ half cross-stitch

Mermaid Locks Scarf
by Tanis Galik

With colors reminiscent of the ocean, this scarf is as cool as an ocean breeze. The textured fringe including the addition of buttons resembles a mermaid's locks.

MATERIALS

1 ball Caron Simply Soft Paints (208 yds/190m) or similar medium weight yarn; shown in color Oceana (A)

Size US I-9 (5.5mm) crochet hook

1 ball Sensations Rainbow Boucle (853 yds/780m) or similar boucle yarn; shown in New Turquoise (B)

56 various small buttons

GAUGE

Gauge is not critical to this project.

1 Crochet the scarf using the pattern below.

With color A, ch 316. End off.

Row 1: With A, ch 10, sk 10 ch on foundation ch, sc in next 296 ch, ch 10. End off.

Row 2: With B, ch 10, working in blo, hdc in each sc, ch 10. End off.

Row 3: With A, ch 10, sc in each hdc, ch 10. End off.

Row 4: With A, ch 10, working in blo, sc in each sc, ch 10. End off.

Repeat rows 2–4 until width measures 5" (12.7cm).

2 Finish the fringe: Tie a knot in a color A fringe end, add a button, and tie another knot after the button. Randomly space 2 small buttons of complementary colors on each strand of color A fringe. Tie the end of each color B fringe strand in a series of knots.

Note

Work on the front side only. Leave 6" (15.2cm) yarn tails at the beginning and end of each row for fringe.

Silver Bracelet

by Barbara Swanson

Paper beads, silver paint and Memory Thread combine to create this fun and easy bracelet. Try the same technique to create a gold sparkle bracelet.

MATERIALS

11 strips of ½" (1.3cm) wide tapered magazine papers, approximately 22" (55.9cm) long*

Cotton swab

Craft glue

Small sea sponge

DMC Color Infusions Memory Thread no. 6210, cut into eleven 2½" (6.4cm) lengths

Silver metallic acrylic paint

Twenty-two 4mm silver glass seed beads

14" (35.6cm) of elastic thread

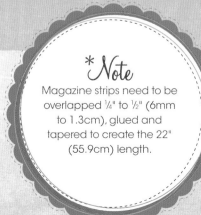

*Note
Magazine strips need to be overlapped ¼" to ½" (6mm to 1.3cm), glued and tapered to create the 22" (55.9cm) length.

1 Cut both ends off the cotton swab, reserving the stick. Roll the tapered magazine strips around the cotton swab stick, starting with the wide end and ending with the tapered point. Glue the tapered point in place. Carefully slide the bead off the stick and repeat to create a total of 11 beads.

2 Lay the paper beads on a plate and use the sponge to dab with silver paint (it's okay to let some of the magazine's text/print show through). Allow the paint to dry.

3 Shape, wrap and glue the Memory Thread around each bead as shown, curling ends in a small swirl.

4 String the paper beads on the elastic as shown, alternating paper beads with 2 glass beads.

5 Knot the ends of the elastic and trim. Dab the knot with glue to secure.

Snoots & Friends Softies
by Susan Layman

Designed with the holiday season in mind, this adorable mouse pattern includes two embroidery designs for red work. You'll definitely want to make more than one!

MATERIALS

12" (30.5cm) square of white cotton fabric (for the body)

12" (30.5cm) square of lightweight iron-on interfacing

6" × 2" (15.2cm × 5.1cm) felt

2" (5.1cm) square of cotton (for the nose)

Polyester fiberfill

6-strand red embroidery floss

Red DMC Pearl Cotton floss, size 5

1 Fuse the interfacing to wrong side of the white cotton fabric. Cut the templates out of paper and position them on the right side of the fabric. Mark location of the embroidery and the marking circles on the wrong sides of the fabric pieces. Cut the pieces out. Place the ear templates on the wrong side of felt, and transfer the markings. Cut out the ears, making sure to keep the right and left ears separate.

2 Make the nose: Center the nose template on the wrong side of the nose fabric. Trace the template. Using a loose gathering stitch, follow the circle outline by hand or machine. Leave "thread tails" to pull for gathering. Pull the bobbin thread gently at both ends so the circles form a pouch. Add filler and close the pouch making small stitches around the

base, catching the gathered pleat. Stitch neatly to completely close the pouch and form a poufy button. Trim the fabric close to the base being careful not to clip your stitches. Position the finished button on the front body piece and hand-stitch in place, fitting it snugly against the fabric.

3 Make the whiskers: Thread needle with 3 strands of floss. Enter at the base of the button and exit on the other side.Knot each side close to the base. Trim the floss to desired whisker length.

4 Embroider: Transfer the embroidery designs to the front body piece using a lightbox or window. Stitch eyes and body design with 2 strands of floss on front body piece.

Complete all stitching and hand sewing to body pieces before assembling. Keep all embroidery designs 1" (2.5cm) above bottom seam line and from the sides ¼" (6mm) seam allowance.

5 Braid the tail: Cut three 5" (12.7cm) lengths of Pearl floss. Knot at one end. Tape or pin to your work surface and braid; knot when you reach the end. Attach to the back body piece. Hand-stitch with floss to secure it. Continue stitching to simulate a bow.

6 Sew on the ears: with right sides together, place the ears on the front body piece, where indicated. Baste ⅛" (3mm) from the seam line to hold ears in place while assembling.

7 With right sides together, sew bottom pieces together, matching A marks and sewing to each corner. Backstitch at beginning and end. This will create a 1½" (3.8cm) bottom opening, securely stitched for turning and stuffing. Press seams open. Sew side panels to bottom piece, matching B marks.

8 Place front and back panels right sides together, matching marks and keeping the tail away from the seam line. Sew from the left D mark, just below the ear location and around to the other D mark. Notch the outward curve and snip the inward curve but not through seams. Press seams open and smooth the curve with your finger.

9 Align and sew the completed side/bottom panel to the front/back panel, matching C, B and D marks. Keep the tail to the center and away from the seam line. Press seams open to smooth areas.

10 Gently pull the mouse through the bottom opening, right-side out. Press, smoothing the seams and stitching.

11 Stuff the mouse, using a stuffing tool as needed. Hand-stitch the bottom closed.

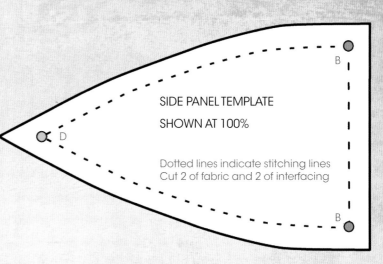

SIDE PANEL TEMPLATE
SHOWN AT 100%

Dotted lines indicate stitching lines
Cut 2 of fabric and 2 of interfacing

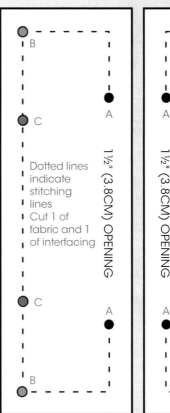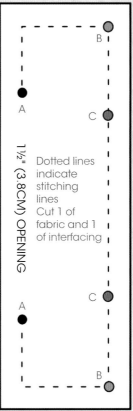

1½" (3.8CM) OPENING

Dotted lines indicate stitching lines
Cut 1 of fabric and 1 of interfacing

BOTTOM PIECE TEMPLATES
SHOWN AT 100%

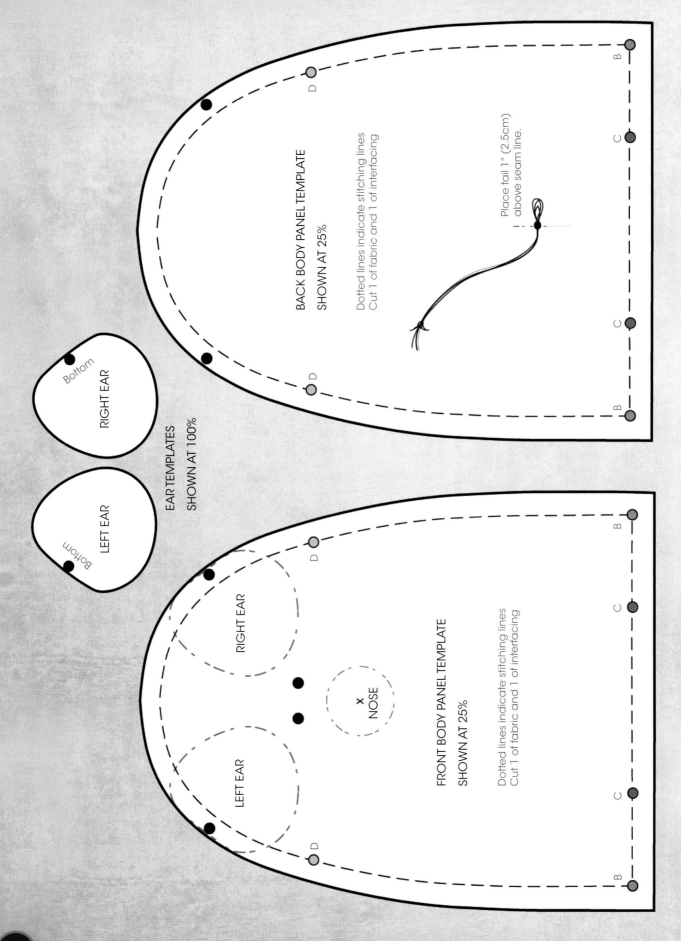

BACK BODY PANEL TEMPLATE
SHOWN AT 25%

Dotted lines indicate stitching lines
Cut 1 of fabric and 1 of interfacing

Place tail 1" (2.5cm) above seam line.

RIGHT EAR

Bottom

LEFT EAR

Bottom

EAR TEMPLATES
SHOWN AT 100%

RIGHT EAR

NOSE

LEFT EAR

FRONT BODY PANEL TEMPLATE
SHOWN AT 25%

Dotted lines indicate stitching lines
Cut 1 of fabric and 1 of interfacing

EMBROIDERY TEMPLATE

SHOWN AT 100%

EMBROIDERY TEMPLATE

SHOWN AT 100%

NOSE TEMPLATE

SHOWN AT 100%

Foxglove Hat
by Linda Browning

Made up of a simple lace pattern, this hat looks much more complicated than it is. For a beret-style hat, use wool yarn and block the wet hat on a large, round plate.

MATERIALS

1 ball Deborah Norville Everyday Soft Worsted (203 yds/186m) or similar medium-weight yarn

Size US 7 (4.50mm) 16" (40.6cm) circular knitting needle or size to obtain gauge

Size US 9 (5.5mm) (or 2 sizes larger than size needed to obtain gauge) 16" (40.6cm) circular needle and douple-pointed needles

Tapestry needle

GAUGE

21 stitches = 4" (10.2cm) in the ribbing stitch on smaller needles

1 Knit the hat using the pattern below.

CO 85 sts very loosely with the larger needle. Being very careful not to twist your stitches, join in the round.

With smaller needles, knit the ribbing section.
Rnds 1-4: (K3, p2) to end of round (85 sts).
Rnd 5: (K2, kfb, p2) to end of round (102 sts).

Switch to larger needles to knit the lace section.
Rnd 6: [K2tog 3 times, (yo, k1) 5 times, yo, k2tog 3 times] to end of round (102 sts).
Rnd 7 (and all odd rnds): K all stitches.
Repeat these 2 rnds 13 times.

Knit the decrease section: switch to DPNs at rnd 40. Arrange 2 repeats of the pattern on each of the 3 DPNs.

Rnd 34: [K2tog 3 times, k1, (yo, k1) 4 times, k2tog 3 times] to end of rnd (90 sts).
Rnd 36: [K2tog 3 times, (yo, k1) 3 times, yo, k2tog 3 times] to end of rnd (78 sts).
Rnd 38: [K2tog 2 times, k2, yo, k1, yo, k2, k2tog 2 times] to end of rnd (66 sts).
Rnd 40: [K2tog 2 times, (k1, yo) 2 times, k1, k2tog 2 times] to end of rnd (54 sts).
Rnd 42: [K2tog 2 times, yo, k1, yo, k2tog 2 times] to end of rnd (42 sts).
Rnd 44: [K2tog, k3, k2tog] to end of rnd (30 sts).
Rnd 46: [K2tog, k1, k2tog] to end of rnd (18 sts).
Rnd 47: Knit.

2 Break of the yarn leaving a long tail. Thread the tail through your tapestry needle and pass the needle and yarn through all 18 sts, removing the sts from the DPNs as you pass through them. Pull yarn tightly to close the hat, and weave in the end.

3 After knitting, wash your hat, and squeeze out the excess water gently. Block your hat in the desired shape.

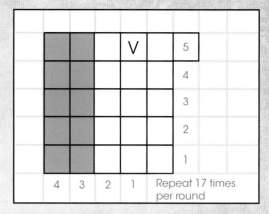

RIBBING CHART

CHART KEY

	K
	P
V	Increase made by kfb
O	YO
⟋	K2tog

LACE CHART

Only RS rows shown
Repeat 6 times per round

Russian Bell Doll
by Anastasia & Marina Popova

The Russian bell doll, *kolokol*, is a traditional Russian doll. The dolls are not just toys for children to play with, but they follow women through their lives, as a companion and protector.

MATERIALS

White, red, green, blue and yellow fabric

Polyester fiberfill

Sewing thread

1 Cut out from the blue fabric an 8¼" (21cm) circle, from the green fabric, a 7½" (19.1cm) circle and from the yellow fabric, a 6¼" (15.9cm) circle. Cut two 7" (17.8cm) squares, one each from the red and the white fabrics.

2 Place the blue circle right-side down on your work surface. Place a small amount of fiberfill in the middle of the circle. Gather the circle up around the stuff and wrap the thread around the fiberfill to create the head.

3 Gather the green circle around the center of the head and secure by wrapping more thread. Repeat with the yellow circle.

4 To form the arms, fold the opposite edges of the white square into the center. Then, fold in half. Tie the ends to create hands.

5 Center the arm piece over the head, unfolding the fabric slightly so it covers the head. Tie in place.

6 Fold the red square diagonally. Place the kerchief on top of the head, wrapping the sides around the neck and tying the ends together in the back.

Unforgettable Greeting Card
by Lisa Swift

Use this beautiful card as a gift to someone special.

MATERIALS

Kraft cardstock

Scrapbook paper with text print

Craft glue

Natural burlap fabric

Rust-colored layered fabric flower

Shipping twine

Medium green button

Sentiment sticker, such as "Unforgettable"

Note
Change the sentiment of your card by using different word stickers. The possibilities are endless!

1 Cut a 8" × 5½" (20.3cm × 14cm) piece of kraft cardstock. Fold in half to create the card base.

2 Cut a 3⅞" × 5⅜" (9.8cm × 13.7cm) piece of text scrapbook paper. Glue to the card front. Cut a 3" (7.6cm) square of burlap fabric and glue it to the center of the scrapbook paper.

3 Glue a large premade fabric flower over the burlap.

4 Thread a 6" (15.2cm) length of shipping twine through the holes of the button and tie the twine into a bow. Glue the button to the flower center. Add a sentiment sticker to the bottom right corner of the card.

Sparkle Heart Pendant
by Christine Lehto

This pendant is a perfect gift for a loved one, or make a bunch and keep one for yourself. Experimenting with alcohol ink on this pendant will allow for endless variations.

MATERIALS

Waxed paper

Olive oil or gloves

¼ lb. (113.4g) Apoxie Sculpt, Natural color

Glitter in color(s) of your choice

Rubber stamp with a texture or pattern

Optional: rubber alphabet stamps

Eye pins

Wire cutters

2-3 colors of alcohol ink (1 color in metallic gold or silver)

Old paintbrush

Clear glaze

Jump ring

1 Cover your work surface with waxed paper. Rub a small drop of olive oil on your hands or use gloves while mixing the Apoxie Sculpt. Roll a ball approximately ½" (1.3cm) in diameter of each part A and part B of the Apoxie, then roll the balls into logs. Twist the logs together to begin mixing the Apoxie. Continue to mix for 2 to 3 minutes.

2 After the Apoxie is thoroughly mixed, shape it into hearts. If the Apoxie is too soft, let it cure slightly (about 15 minutes) before continuing. Use water to smooth out the Apoxie as you work as necessary.

3 Once the heart is shaped, rub the glitter over the surface of 1 side of the heart with your fingertip. To add a second color, leave portions of the heart uncovered, and rub the second color over these uncovered areas.

4 On your work surface, place the textured rubber stamp with the rubber side facing up. Position your heart piece onto the rubber stamp with the glittered side facing down. Lightly press the heart piece into the stamp to make an impression.

To make an initial on your heart, press the letter stamp of your choice into the heart when it is covering the textured rubber stamp surface.

5 When you are happy with how your heart looks, carefully insert an eye pin into the heart. Depending on the size of your heart and the length of your eye pin, you may need to trim the eye pin using wire cutters before inserting it into the heart.

6 Carefully place your heart glittered side down onto a piece of waxed paper. Allow the heart to cure for at least 3 hours.

7 Once the heart has hardened, add the alcohol ink to the unglittered side of the heart. Place a drop of ink onto the bare surface of the heart. Add a drop of a metallic color while the first color is still wet. Swirl the colors together. Use an old paintbrush to ensure the ink covers the entire surface. Let the ink dry.

8 Once the ink is dry, apply a clear glaze to protect the surface. Add a jump ring to the eye pin on the heart. It is now ready to wear as a pendant.

Flower Power Tote
by Sharon Madsen

Turn a plain straw tote into a bloomin' beauty with button and fabric flower embellishments.

MATERIALS

Fabric scraps to cover the buttons

Nine 1½" (3.8cm) covered button blanks

Purchased straw tote

Fabric marker

7 yds (6.4m) of 1" (2.5cm) double-fold bias tape (store-bought or handmade)

Coordinating thread

Craft glue

Embroidery thread

1 Cut nine 2½" (6.4cm) diameter fabric circles. Following the manufacturer's directions, cover the button blanks.

2 On the front side of the tote, arrange the buttons in an even pattern of 3 across and 3 down. Using a fabric marker, draw a small circle on the tote where the center of each button is located. Remove the buttons and set aside.

3 Cut the bias tape into 72 pieces each 3½" (8.9cm) long.

4 To create the flower petals, fold 8 bias tape pieces in half, wrong sides together and matching short raw edges. Position the petals in a circle around a marked circle on the tote. Hand-stitch or glue in place. Repeat for remaining flowers.

5 Position a covered button over the center of each set of petals covering the raw edges. Hand stitch or glue the buttons to the tote.

6 Using a contrasting embroidery thread, stitch a row of running stitches around the perimeter of each covered button, securing the petals to the tote.

Decorative Bottles
by Ashley Mary Dunlop

Transform glass bottles into a fun, creative and inexpensive craft that you can easily personalize. Use these decorative bottles as flower vases, home decor and at celebrations as centerpieces.

MATERIALS

Glass bottles (beer and wine bottles work well)

Tape measure

Fabric scraps (to wrap bottles)

Hot glue gun and glue sticks

Jute twine (3 ply)

1 Wash bottles with soap and warm water and scrub away any labels with a stainless steel scourer for easy removal.

2 Measure each bottle's height and circumference with a tape measure. (Do not include the neck of the bottle in your measurements, it is wrapped with jute string.) Use these dimensions to cut out fabric for each bottle.

3 Glue the fabric onto the bottles. Cover the fabric overlap or where the fabric meets on the body of the bottle with a piece of jute string. Wrap a piece of jute string around the bottom circumference of the bottle for a more tailored look. Apply additional pieces of jute string as desired.

4 Begin wrapping the jute string around the neck of the bottle, gluing in place as you wrap. Wrap the jute tightly so no spaces or gaps show. Be careful not to burn your fingers when using the hot glue gun. Continue wrapping the jute until the bottle neck is completely covered.

Scandinavian Retro Tissue Pouch

by Kajsa Kinsella

Easy to make and oh-so practical, this tissue pouch is just the thing to add a touch of style in an unexpected place.

MATERIALS

Orange, black, red and green felt

Black, red and green thread

Tissues

1 Cut the orange felt into a 3" × 6" (7.6cm × 15.2cm) rectangle. Use the templates to cut a large circle out of black felt, a small circle out of red, and a stem and 2 leaves out of green.

2 Lay the green stem on the orange rectangle with the top of the stem at the vertical center of the rectangle. Arrange the black circle on top of the stem and the red circle on top of the black. Place the leaves high up on the stem.

3 Attach all parts of the flower with a sewing machine or by hand using the corresponding thread colors.

4 Load your sewing machine with red thread and sew along the short sides of the rectangle, ⅖" (1cm) from the edge.

5 With the rectangle facedown, place a tissue in the center and fold the shorter sides of the black felt (the sides with red stitching) over to meet in the middle. Sew along open side seams, going slowly so the seams don't slide apart.

6 Sew a second side seam, just inside the first. Use pinking shears to trim the felt on the side seams, being careful not to cut your stitches.

LARGE CIRCLE TEMPLATE
SHOWN AT 100%

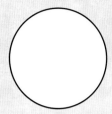

SMALL CIRCLE TEMPLATE
SHOWN AT 100%

LEAF TEMPLATE
SHOWN AT 100%

Cut 2

STEM TEMPLATE
SHOWN AT 100%

Pretty Little Collar
by *Kathy North*

Delicate looking but easy to stitch, this lace collar provides a touch of vintage flair in a contemporary world.

MATERIALS

1 ball Patons Grace (136 yds/125m) or similar light-weight cotton yarn

Size US E/4 (3.5mm) crochet hook, or size needed to achieve gauge

One ⅜" (9.5mm) button

Tapestry needle

GAUGE

19 dc and 10 rows = 4" (10.2cm) on size US E/4 (3.5mm) hook

Notes

The collar is worked in rows from narrow end to narrow end, then chain loop edging is added.

Beginning chain counts as a stitch.

1 Crochet the collar using the pattern below.

Row 1: Ch 20, tc in 4th ch from hk, tc in ea of next 3 ch, dc in ea of next 4 ch, hdc in ea of next 4 ch, sc in each of last 5 ch, turn (18 sts).

Row 2: Ch 3, dc in next sc, *ch 1, sk next st, dc in next st, rep from * across, ending with dc in top of turning ch, turn (10 dc, 9 sps).

Row 3: Ch 4, tc in first sp, tc in next dc, tc in next sp, tc in next dc, (dc in next sp, dc in next dc) twice, (hdc in next sp, hdc in next dc) twice, (sc in next sp, sc in next dc) twice, sc in top of turning ch, turn (18 sts).

Rep rows 2–3 until piece measures 19" (48.3cm) from beg along neckline curve. At the end of the last row, do not turn but pivot piece to work along neckline edge.

2 Working evenly around entire piece, ch 5, sl st in same st at base of beg ch-5 (button loop completed), *ch 5, sl st in end of next dc/sp row, rep from * across to corner, pivot piece to work along narrow front edge; *ch 5, sk next 2 sts, sl st in next st, rep from * to next corner, pivot piece to work along curved outer edge; *ch 5, sl st in end of next row (i.e., ch 5, sl st in each tc row end and each dc/sp row end), rep from * to next corner, pivot piece to work along narrow front edge; *ch 5, sk next 2 sts, sl st in next st, rep from * across, join with sl st at base of beg ch-5.

Fasten off and weave in tails.

3 Sew the button to the opposite end of the piece in line with the button loop.

Snowman Bookmark
by Izzy Anderson

This bookmark would be perfect tucked into a winter-themed book. It's a great gift for any reader and is quick and inexpensive to make.

MATERIALS

Patterned paper scraps*

White doily

Snowman sticker

Sentiment stickers

Twine tassel

*Note

I used paper and stickers from Echo Park Paper (the Holly Jolly collection).

1 Choose 2 coordinating pieces of patterned paper. Cut 1 piece 1½" × 6" (3.8cm × 15.2cm) and the other slightly smaller.

2 Layer the smaller piece on top of the larger piece and stitch the two together to form the base of the bookmark.

3 Fold over a small white doily (to resemble a snowball) and place the snowman sticker on top. Add the sentiment stickers.

4 Make a tassel from twine or attach a premade one.

5 Punch hole in the top of the bookmark and loop the tassel through to attach.

Romantic Color Block Scarf
by *Sharon Madsen*

Give your outfit a romantic touch with this lacy scarf.

MATERIALS

⅔ yd (60.4cm) lightweight silk (solid)

⅔ yd (60.4cm) lightweight cotton voile (print)

1 yd (91.4cm) 9" (22.9cm) flat lace

2 yds (1.8m) 2" (5.1cm) wide Venice lace

2 yds (1.8m) 4" (10.2cm) wide flat lace

Coordinating thread

1 Cut two 36" × 6" (91.4cm × 15.2cm) and four 36" × 2" (91.4cm × 5.1cm) rectangles of silk. Cut two 36" × 12" (91.4cm × 30.5cm) rectangles of cotton voile. Cut the 9" (22.9cm) wide lace in half, creating two ½ yd (45.7cm) pieces.

2 Stitch the 36" × 6" (91.4cm × 15.2cm) silk rectangles together using a French seam. To stitch the French seam, position the silk rectangles wrong sides together matching 1 short edge; stitch using a ⅛" (3mm) seam allowance. Press the seam toward one side. Turn the fabric right sides together and press the seam. Stitch again using a ⅜" (1cm) seam allowance to encase the raw edge; press seam to 1 side. Stitch the 36" × 2" (91.4cm × 5.1cm) silk rectangles together using a French seam to create 1 long strip. Stitch the 36" × 12" (91.4cm × 30.5cm) cotton voile rectangles together along one short edge using a French seam.

3 Serge-finish all 4 edges of each fabric rectangle and the long silk strip. Alternately, double fold all 4 edges ¼" (6mm) toward the wrong side; press, and then stitch.

4 With wrong sides together, stitch the silk and cotton voile rectangles (now 72" [1.8m] long) along 1 long edge using a ½" (1.3cm) seam allowance; press open.

5 Stitch a row of basting stitches along the center of the long silk strip leaving long thread tails on each end. Stitch a second row of basting stitches ⅛" (3mm) away leaving long thread tails. Gently pull on the thread tails to evenly gather the strip until it measures 72" (1.8m).

6 Stitch a row of basting stitches 1" (2.5cm) from the upper edge of each 9" (22.9cm) wide lace leaving long thread tails. Stitch a second row of basting stitches ⅛" (3mm) away leaving long thread tails. Gently gather the lace to the width of the scarf ends. Repeat with the other 9" (22.9cm) piece of lace.

7 Lay the scarf right side up. Pin the silk ruffle strip on the voile section 6" (15.2cm) from the long edge; stitch in place. Pin the 4" (10.2cm) wide flat lace next to the seam joining the silk and voile; stitch in place. Position the Venice lace on top of the lace you just stitched in place; pin and stitch in place. Pin the gathered lace along each lower-edge of the scarf; stitch in place.

Batik Wall Decoration
by Dian K. Wardhani

A beautiful combination of batik and felt, this simple project turns ordinary felt into antique-inspired wall decor.

MATERIALS

Fusible webbing

Scraps of cotton batik fabric

Scraps of felt

Thin foam or cardboard

Embroidery floss

3 buttons made from coconut shell

2 wooden flowers

Bronze tassel

2 bronze beads

1 Iron the fusible webbing onto the cotton batik following the manufacturer's directions.

2 Using the templates, cut out 2 cotton circles, 1 felt circle, 1 cotton square and 2 felt squares. Cut 3 squares from the foam or cardboard.

3 Place a felt circle facedown. Layer a foam square on top and cover with a fabric square. Fold the circle around the square and press with an iron. Blanket-stitch around the edge of the circle with embroidery floss. Optional: Sew a running stitch on square, tracing the shape of the circle.

Repeat with the remaining circles and squares, alternating fabric and felt circles and squares.

4 Sew a coconut shell button in the middle of each square.

5 Arrange your squares corner to corner, placing a wooden flower at the point where the diamonds connect. Using embroidery floss, sew the flowers in place, joining the diamonds as you go.

6 Attach the tassle to a bronze bead and sew the bead onto the bottom of point of the bottom square. Sew the remaining bronze bead to the top, leaving a hoop for hanging.

CIRCLE TEMPLATE

SHOWN AT 100%

Cut 2 from cotton
Cut 1 from felt

SQUARE TEMPLATE

SHOWN AT 50%

Cut 2 from felt
Cut 1 from cotton

Thank You Bags
by Denise Lavoie

Nothing says "thank you" like a great gift thoughtfully wrapped. Use luscious yarn for a special occasion or stash-bust for those unexpected, last minute gifts.

MATERIALS

1 skein Neighborhood Fiber Co. Penthouse Silk (500 yds/455m) or similar super-fine-weight yarn; shown in color Victorian Village

Size US E-4 (3.5mm) and steel US 12 (1mm) crochet hooks

4 yds × ¼" (3.7m × 6mm) pink organdy ribbon, cut into ½yd (45.7cm) lengths

10g size 6 round silver-lined transparent beads; shown in light rose

GAUGE

21 stitches × 20 rows = 4" (10.2cm) on US E-4 (3.5mm) hook

FINISHED DIMENSIONS

6" × 9" (15.2cm × 22.9cm)
9" × 12" (22.9cm × 30.5cm)

Note
Pattern for the larger bag is in parentheses.

1 Crochet the bags using the pattern below.

With larger hook, chain 27 (39).
Row 1: Sc in 2nd ch from hk, *sc in next ch, tc in next ch. Repeat from * across row, ending with sc in final 2 chs. Turn (26 [38] stitches).

Repeat the stitch pattern until piece measures 14" (35.6cm) (18" [45.7cm]).

Stitch Pattern
Row 1: Ch 1, sc in next st (selvage st), *tc in next st, sc in next st. Repeat from * across row, with final ch 1 acting as selvage st. Turn.
Row 2: Ch 1, sc in next st (selvage st), *sc in next st, tc in next st. Repeat from * across row until 2 sts remain, sc in each of last 2 sts. Turn.

2 Fold the bag in half widthwise, wrong sides out, and seam the long sides. Weave in the ends, and turn the bag right-side out.

3 With the smaller steel hook, string 26 (38) beads onto yarn. With the larger hook, attach yarn with sl st at top right edge, pulling hook from RS to WS. *Ch 1, pull up 1 bead, ch 2, sk next st, sc in next st. Repeat from * around top of bag until 2 sts remain, ending with ch 1, pull up 1 bead, ch 2, sk next st, sl st in initial ch 1. Fasten off and weave in ends.

4 Starting at the left side seam 1" (2.5cm) from the top, weave a piece of ribbon in and out of tc spaces, then knot the ends. Repeat with right side.

Polka Dot Coaster
by Janet Brani

Turn your old wool sweaters into coasters with this simple project.

MATERIALS

Old wool sweater (for felting)

Cotton crochet thread, size 10

Sharp crochet hook*

*Note

I use the Sharp Crochet Hook (www.sharpcrochethook.com) to crochet directly into the wool, but you can use a steel crochet hook (size US 6 [1.8mm] or 7 [1.65mm]), as well. If the hook does not easily pierce the felt, use a darning needle to make holes for the stitches in round 1.

1 Felt the wool sweater by washing on a long setting in hot soapy water. Toss in a couple of old pairs of jeans to aid in the agitation. Dry completely in the dryer.

2 Cut a 3½" (8.9cm) circle from the sweater.

3 Crochet the border using the pattern below.

Rnd 1: Insert the Sharp Crochet Hook about ³⁄₁₆" (5mm) from the circle edge and pull a loop of crochet thread through. Ch1, sc into the same space, ch 3, sc about ¼" (6mm) from the first sc. Continue around the circle, equally spacing the single crochet stitches and making 3 chs between each. Join with a sl st to first sc made.

Rnd 2: Ch 1, 3 sc into each ch-3 space around. Join with a sl st to first sc of round.

4 Fasten off and weave in ends.

Sewing Techniques

Basic Stitches

When sewing by hand, choose a needle that matches the thickness of the thread you are using so the thread passes easily through the fabric. All stitches can be started with a knot on the back of the work and finished off neatly at the back, usually with backstitch.

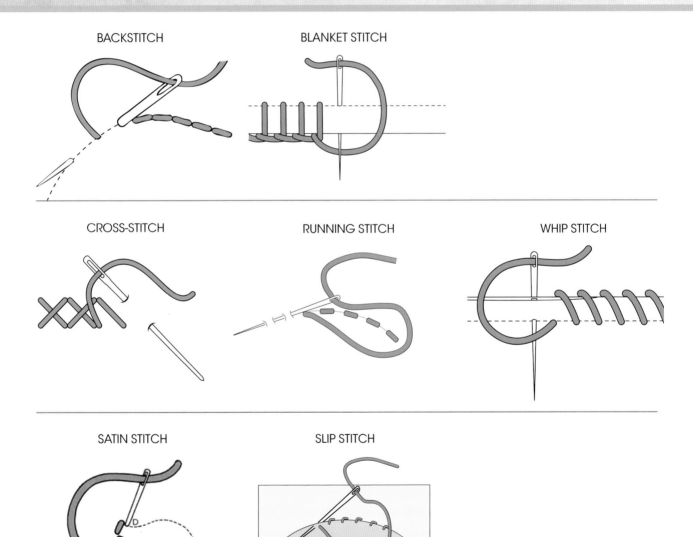

BACKSTITCH

BLANKET STITCH

CROSS-STITCH

RUNNING STITCH

WHIP STITCH

SATIN STITCH

SLIP STITCH

Knitting and Crochet Basics

Abbreviations

approx – approximately
beg – beginning
blo – back loop only
ch – chain
dc – double crochet
dec – decrease
dpn(s) – double-pointed needles
hdc – half double crochet
inc – increase

k – knit
kfb – knit in the front and back of the stitch
p – purl
rem – remaining
rep – repeat
rnd(s) – rounds
RS – right side
sc – single crochet

sc dec – single crochet decrease
sk – skip
sl – slip
sl st – slip stitch
St st – Stockinette stitch
tc – treble crochet
tog – together
WS – wrong side
yo – yarn over

Notes

*Gauge is measured over 4" (10cm) in single crochet.

**Gauge is measured over 4" (10cm) in stockinette stitch.

***Steel crochet hooks are sized differently from regular hook—the higher the number, the smaller the hook, which is the reverse of regular hook sizing.

Yarn Weight Guidelines

Names given to different weights of yarn can vary depending on the country of origin or the yarn manufacturer's preference. The Craft Yarn Council of America has created a standard yarn weight system to bring order to yarn labels. Look for a picture of a skein of yarn with a number 0–6 on most kinds of yarn to figure out its *official* weight. The information below is taken from www.yarnstandards.com.

	0 LACE	1 SUPER FINE	2 FINE	3 LIGHT	4 MEDIUM	5 BULKY	6 SUPER BULKY
Weight	fingering, 10-count crochet thread	sock, fingering, 2-ply, 3-ply	sport, baby, 4-ply	light worsted, DK	worsted, afghan, aran	chunky, craft, rug	super-chunky, bulky, roving
Crochet Gauge Range*	32–42 sts	21–32 sts	16–20 sts	12–17 sts	11–14 sts	8–11 sts	5–9 sts
Recommended Hook Range	Steel*** 6, 7, 8 Regular hook B/1 (1.4mm–2.25mm)	B/1 to E/4 (2.25mm–3.5mm)	E/4 to 7 (3.5mm–4.5mm)	7 to I/9 (4.5mm–5.5mm)	I/9 to K/10½ (5.5mm–6.5mm)	K/10½ to M/13 (6.5mm–9mm)	M/13 and larger (9mm and larger)
Knit Gauge Range**	33–40 sts	27–32 sts	23–26 sts	21–24 sts	16–20 sts	12–15 sts	6–11 sts
Recommended Needle Range	000 to 1 (2mm–2.5mm)	1 to 3 (2.25mm–3.25mm)	3 to 5 (3.25mm–3.75mm)	5 to 7 (3.75mm–4.5mm)	7 to 9 (4.5mm–5.5mm)	9 to 11 (5.5mm–8mm)	11 (8mm) and larger

Crochet Techniques

Crochet Terms Used in This Book

Be aware that some crochet terms in the UK are different from those in the US. This book uses US terms. Please refer to the charts for UK terms.

US CROCHET TERM	UK CROCHET TERM
chain	chain
slip stitch	slip stitch
single crochet	double crochet
half double crochet	half treble
double crochet	treble
treble crochet	double treble

SLIPKNOT

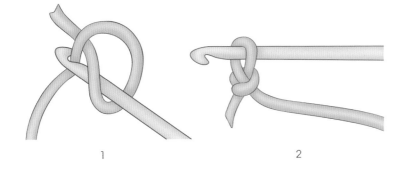

1

2

CHAIN

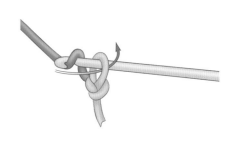

SINGLE CROCHET

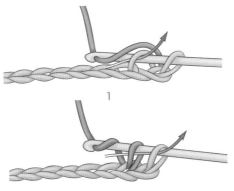

1

2

SLIP STITCH

Crochet Techniques

DOUBLE CROCHET

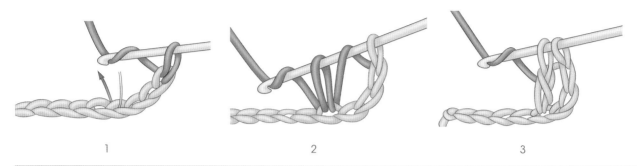

1   2   3

TREBLE CROCHET

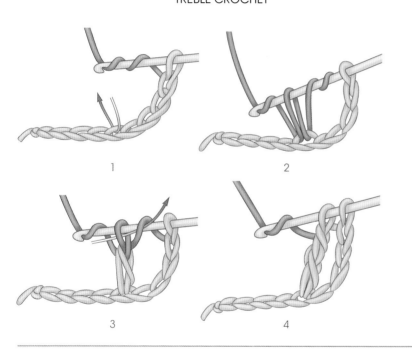

1   2

3   4

HALF DOUBLE CROCHET

CHANGING COLORS

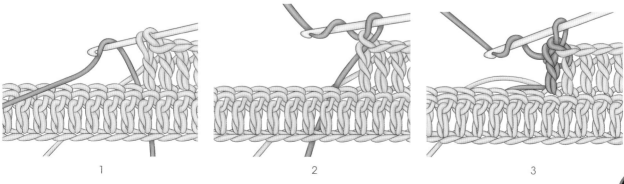

1   2   3

Knitting Techniques

Knitting Terms Used in This Book

Be aware that some knitting terms in the UK are different from those in the US. This book uses US terms. Please refer to the charts for UK terms.

US KNITTING TERM	UK KNITTING TERM
bind off	cast off
gauge	tension
Stockinette stitch	stocking stitch
reverse Stockinette stitch	reverse stocking stitch
seed stitch	moss stitch

CAST ON

KNIT STITCH

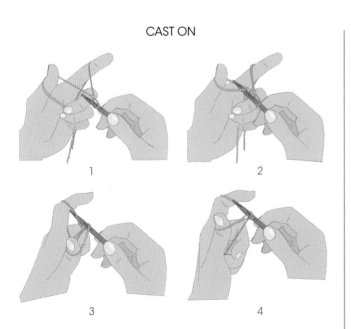

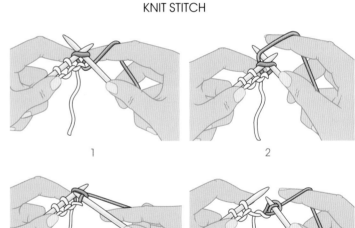

PURL STITCH

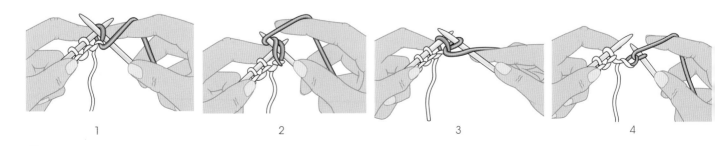

Knitting Techniques

KITCHENER STITCH

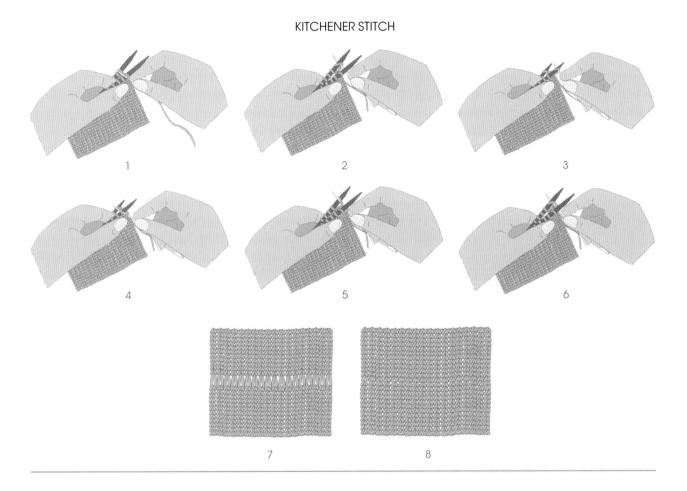

1   2   3

4   5   6

7   8

K2TOG   ## P2TOG

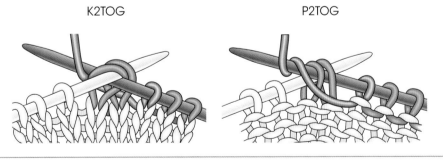

BINDING OFF

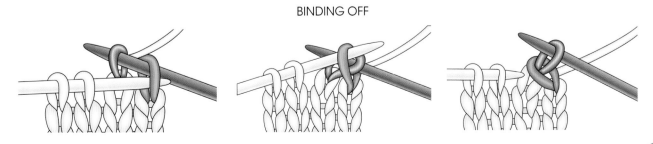

Contributors

Andretta Ross makes custom wreaths. See her full line of designs at www.WreathinkGifting.com or www.WreathinkGifting.etsy.com.

Angela Davis is a Craft Yarn Council of America certified hand knitting instructor. Find her at alittlebirdwithyarn.wordpress.com.

Anne Glynis Davies is a UK-based artist, author and teacher who works in textiles and mixed media. Find her work at www.anneglynisdavies.com/ and artandlovely.blogspot.co.uk/.

Ashley Mary Dunlop runs her own etsy shop, www.heart2homecreations.etsy.com, and blog, www.fromhearttohomecreations.blogspot.com.

Barbara Gaddy has been designing patterns for the last four years. Find her designs at www.bejeweledquilts.etsy.com, and www.bejeweledquilts.blogspot.com.

Barbara Swanson is an independent designer. Her work includes cross-stitch, embroidery, sewing, quilting, stenciling, paper crafting and more.

Benetta Strydom is from Pretoria, South Africa. She is an avid crafter and enjoys experimenting with different craft media. She has also taken art classes for a few years.

Beth Major has been an avid crocheter for the past thirty years. Visit her etsy shop at www.CrochetGypsy.etsy.com.

Cannon-Marie Milby is an attorney, writer and an independent designer. Visit her Etsy shop, www.hollyandalder.etsy.com.

Cheryl Bush is a self-taught crafter with designs in numerous publications. Visit her blog, www.sewcando.com and etsy shop, www.thegreenhedgehog.com.

Christen Barber is a designer and owner of www.love-elaine.com, a handmade shop that features unique gifts. Visit her new creative blog, www.lovebyhand.com.

Christine Lehto is passionate about sculpting, paper crafting and watercolor. Visit her etsy shop, www.lillybugboutique.etsy.com.

Courtney Kyle is the former Senior Designer for *Stitch Craft Create* magazine and is currently a freelance graphic designer. Find her at www.courtneykyle.com.

Dalia Torres comes from a line of crafters. Visit her shop, www.inspirationsbyd.etsy.com, and blog, www.inspirationsbyd.com for more information.

Danielle Branch is a long-time crocheter who recently turned her attention to blogging. Visit her blog, www.DanidoesDoilies.blogspot.com.

Denise Lavoie is a published knit- and crochet-wear designer and painter. Visit her blog, http://voiedevie.blogspot.com, to see more of her designs and paintings.

Dian K. Wardhani is a craft book author and children's book illustrator. Visit her at www.capungmungil.weebly.com.

Doris Lovadina-Lee has been sewing and quilting for many years. She recently began to publish patterns. Visit www.dorislovadinalee.com to see her work.

Ellyn Zinsmeister is a pattern designer, seamstress and blogger who loves bright colors, rickrack and polka dots. You can find her online at www.ellynsplace.com.

Izumi Ouchi designs for knitting magazines and books and teaches Ipponbari knitting in Japan. Visit her blog, somethingy.exblog.jp.

Izzy Anderson is a freelance designer currently on the creative team for Fancy Pants Designs. Visit her blog, www.izzyanderson.com.

Janet Brani is a published crochet designer and instructor. Visit her shops on Ravelry or Etsy, and check out her website at www.oneloopshy.com.

Joy Neihaus is a self-taught sewist. She sells handmade dolls at www.thegoosebearyshop.etsy.com. Visit her blog, www.redirecteddreams.blogspot.com.

Kajsa Kinsella is a busy Swede who runs her own craft business and bakery. Her creations reflect classic Scandinavian style. Find her at www.thenorthernshores.com.

Kathy North is a published designer whose work has appeared in books and magazines. Visit her at www.designsbykn.com or on Ravelry (ID: dbkn5).

Contributors

Katie Smith is a published designer, most recently featured in *The Star Trek Craft Book* (Pocket Books, 2013). Find her at www.punkprojects.com or www.punkprojects.etsy.com.

Kim Harrington is a licensed Martha Pullen instructor, teaching sewing and felting in her local community. She is currently working on new projects.

Linda Browning is a published knitting pattern designer specializing in lace knitting. Find her on Ravelry as Tinyknit, or visit her website, tinyknit.com.

Lisa Swift is a freelance craft designer. See more of her work on her blog, Remember the Good Times (http://lisarukinswift.com).

Lynn Hedgecock has been a crafter since an early age. She is on the board of the Bead Society in NC. Visit her shop at LHJewelryDesign.artfire.com.

Anastasia & Marina Popova are a mother-daughter team. Marina is a professional seamstress who is now using her passion to teach kids to sew. Anastasia is a published crochet designer. Visit her at anastasiapopova.com.

Melissa McLawhorn creates one-of-a-kind jewelry from salvaged materials such as paper, wire, glass, or anything she can cut, break or shred. Visit her etsy shop, www.salvagedjewelry.com.

Melissa Zbikowski has been designing crochet and crafts items for more than six years. Visit her blog, www.thisgirlcreates.com, or etsy shop www.hooksandwhiskers.etsy.com.

Melony Miller-Bradley is a full-time creative designer, publishing original designs in a variety of magazines. Visit her etsy shop at www.melonybradley.etsy.com.

Niki Meiners is a professional designer, specializing in polymer clay, mixed media and papercraft. Visit her at www.sculpey.com/blog/niki.

Paula Ginder is passionate about sewing and crafting. Visit her blog, www.ginderellas.com or her etsy shop, www.ginderellas.etsy.com.

Salena Baca is a published crochet designer and the founder of Design Wars, a popular crochet challenge. For more information, visit www.designwars.com.

Shannon Miller is an editor and designer for *Sew Beautiful* magazine and former editor of *Stitch Craft Create* magazine. Visit her blog at www.craftyinalabama.com.

Sharon Madsen writes patterns and tutorials for her blog, sharonsews.blogspot.com. She's also a contributor to *Sew News* and *Sew it All* magazine.

Sheryl Hastings is a contributor to *Crafts N Things* magazine. Visit her website, www.sherscreativespace.com and her pattern shop, www.sherspatternshop.etsy.com.

Stacy Schyler writes for her blog, www.stacysews.com, devoted to her crafting adventures. She also serves as a sewing expert for Bernina's We All Sew website.

Susan Layman is a graphic artist who loves to draw and write sewing patterns. She lives in Maryland with her husband and sweet little black cat.

Tanis Galik is a published crochet designer. Visit her website, www.interlockingcrochet.com, for video tutorials and to read her blog.

Tara Cousins recently began selling and publishing crochet patterns. Visit her website, www.cutekidscrochet.com, or etsy shop, www.2littlelambscrochet.etsy.com.

Vicki Riggan is a lampwork glass bead artist and jewelry designer. Her jewelry has been featured in local several shops as well in art fairs throughout the tri-state area.

Index

Published by KP Craft, an imprint of F+W Media, Inc., 10151 Carver Road, Suite 200, Blue Ash, Ohio 45242. (800) 289-0963. First Edition.

www.fwmedia.com

18 17 16 15 14   5 4 3 2 1

DISTRIBUTED IN CANADA BY FRASER DIRECT
100 Armstrong Avenue
Georgetown, ON, Canada L7G 5S4
Tel: (905) 877-4411

DISTRIBUTED IN THE U.K. AND EUROPE BY F&W MEDIA INTERNATIONAL
Brunel House, Newton Abbot, Devon, TQ12 4PU, England
Tel: (+44) 1626 323200, Fax: (+44) 1626 323319
Email: enquiries@fwmedia.com

DISTRIBUTED IN AUSTRALIA BY CAPRICORN LINK
P.O. Box 704, S. Windsor NSW, 2756 Australia
Tel: (02) 4560-1600   Fax: 02-4577-5288
Email: books@capricornlink.com.au

SRN: U7283
ISBN-13: 978-1-4402-3824-6

Editor: Stephanie White
Project Manager: Noel Rivera
Designer: Kelly Pace
Photographer: Steven Siedentopf of *Luna Root Studio*
Stylist: Lauren Siedentopf of *Luna Root Studio*
Production Coordinator: Greg Nock

METRIC CONVERSION CHART

To convert	to	multiply by
Inches	Centimeters	2.54
Centimeters	Inches	0.4
Feet	Centimeters	30.5
Centimeters	Feet	0.03
Yards	Meters	0.9
Meters	Yards	1.1

More crafty inspiration awaits!

101 Ways to Stitch Craft Create Vintage

Quick and Easy Projects to Make for Your Vintage Lifestyle
Various Contributors

Be inspired to get crafting with this fun collection of 101 unique vintage-themed projects. Create stunning crafts for yourself or as gifts for friends and family, with a huge selection of vintage projects to choose from, including a vintage button necklace, suffolk puff rings, fondant fancies, fabric pin cushion, crochet hot water bottle cover, and vintage tea stand. This stunning collection of craft projects will inspire you to stitch, craft and create your very own vintage lifestyle!

The Crafter's Book of Clever Ideas

Awesome Craft Techniques for Handmade Craft Projects
Andrea Currie & Cliff Currie

Andrea and Cliff Currie give you 25 fun projects with his and hers variations for a total of 50 unique gift giving and craft party ideas. Try clever techniques with a wide range of materials, including glitter, glass, felt and glue gun resin. Pick projects to make at parties or throw your own shindig with the mosaic partyware, confetti popper and booby-trapped gifts! There's something for every occasion with plenty left over for crafting fun at home.